MEDICAL ADVERTISING HALL OF FAME

The
Story of
Medical
Advertising
in
America

CREDITS:

Art direction Michael J. Lyons

Interior book design Michael J. Lyons *and* Howard R. Roberts

Text composition HRoberts Design

Cover design Michael J. Lyons

Calligraphy Tom Carnese

Production Howard R. Roberts

Editing by the Publication Committee of The Medical Advertising Hall of Fame

Research John Kallir, William G. Castagnoli

Text written by William G. Castagnoli

Additional text written by Frank Hughes, John Kallir, and Ron Pantello

Published by:
The Medical Advertising Hall of Fame
P.O. Box 1028
Huntington, NY 11743-0640

ISBN: 0-9667793-0-4

Library of Congress Catalog Card Number: 98-68323

Printed in Hong Kong

Contents

Acknowledgments

THE PEOPLE WHO CREATED MEDICINE AVENUE

Medicine Avenue is made possible by the contribution of time and financial support from the members of the Executive Committee of the Medical Advertising Hall of Fame. The Publication Committee of the MAHF managed all activities concerning Medicine Avenue. Its members are William G. Castagnoli, Frank Hughes, John Kallir, Michael J. Lyons and Ron Pantello.

The design of Medicine Avenue was created by Mr. Lyons. The introductory preface was written by Kallir, Hughes, and Pantello. Mr. Castagnoli served as overall coordinator and also researched and wrote the historical sections.

The committee wishes to thank all those who contributed information, materials and guidance in putting the book together. Medicine Avenue would never have existed were it not for the foresight of John Kallir and Dick Jones in assembling and preserving the work of medical advertising's Golden Age—the boom years of the 1950's to 1960's. The industry owes them appreciative applause for compiling this archive and making it available. The book, likewise, would not have come to pass if Ron Pantello had not energetically proposed and championed it to the Executive Committee as an important activity for the MAHF in addition to its annual election and award dinner at which leaders of medical advertising are honored.

Many persons supplied information on the history of medical advertising or facilitated our research: Mickey Smith opened the library of the Pharmacy School of the University of Mississippi to us. Brendon and Roderic Phibbs recalled family history, helping us reconstruct the early days of their father's agency, Harry C. Phibbs Advertising Co. Robert Kennett of the AMA assisted in leading us to the Dr. Morris Fishbein Papers at the University of Chicago. Bill Noonan enabled us to obtain IMS data from the past. Vernon Lewis of Medical Economics allowed us to seek out historic ads in their archive. Helping with names, dates, facts and perspectives on events were John Kallir, Joseph Stettler, Irwin Gerson, Ken Gurian, Steve Chappell, Mark Dresden, Bob Baldini, Irwin Lerner, James Dougherty, David Gideon, Rolf Rosenthal, Todd Mahony, Clay Warrington, Bob Buechert, Glenn DeSimone, Dick Jones, John Jones and Ron Wilson.

Special thanks goes to Ina Kramer who made available materials from Rx Club yearbooks, and to Clark-O'Neill and Herb Day for their help in warehousing and distributing Medicine Avenue. And lastly, our appreciation to the medical agencies that submitted work for this retrospective of our business. Thank you, for seeing the value of preserving the heritage of medical advertising.

Medical Advertising Hall of Fame Executive Committee—1998

RON PANTELLO

Chairperson

Lally McFarland & Pantello

EURO RSCG

JED BEITLER

Sudler & Hennessey

DARIA BLACKWELL

Dugan/Farley

MORGAN E. CLINE

Cline Davis & Mann

GLENN DeSIMONE

Medicus Group International

TOM DOMANICO

FCB Healthcare

M. JAMES DOUGHERTY

McGraw-Hill Healthcare Information Group

PHILIP T. BRADY

CommonHealth USA

JOHN J. FISHER

Corbett HealthConnect

SANDER A. FLAUM

Robert A. Becker

EURO RSCG

IRWIN C. GERSON

Lowe McAdams

DAVID GIDEON

Medical Marketing & Media

FRANK HUGHES

GHBM Healthworld

MICHAEL J. LYONS

Lyons Lavey Nickel Swift

C. TODD MAHONY

Integrated Communications

GAVIN A. SCOTTI

Klemtner Advertising

HARRY A. SWEENEY JR.

Dorland Sweeney Jones

LYNN O'CONNOR VOS

Grey Healthcare

RON WILSON

Harrison Wilson

MEDICAL ADVERTISING HALL OF FAME

Foreword

The Medical Advertising Hall of Fame is pleased to present our first publication, *Medicine Avenue: The Story of Medical Advertising in America*.

This book is dedicated to all the men and women who have and are applying their unique intellectual capital to the creation of responsible, creative healthcare advertising. The Medical Advertising Hall of Fame was founded in 1996 for the purpose of recording the history of medical advertising and to honor those individuals who have created this relatively young industry.

As the early founders in the business have passed on or retired, it became evident that efforts were necessary to capture the culture of the industry before that culture was lost. Historically, the medical advertising business was comprised of a homogeneous group of professionals learning their craft on the job. Today's medical advertising business is composed of a heterogeneous group of professionals from varied backgrounds making a multi-disciplined contribution to our business. It is the Medical Advertising Hall of Fame's fervent belief that given this new diversity, it is time to capture the first words and pictures that made our industry great.

It is with this in mind that the Medical Advertising Hall of Fame proudly presents *Medicine Avenue: The Story of Medical Advertising in America*.

Ron Pantello

Chairperson
Executive Committee
Medical Advertising Hall of Fame

The Creative Product

Medicine *Avenue* is a history and also a celebration of the creative product. The authors of this publication took it upon themselves to identify some of the most distinguished advertising of the 50's, 60's, 70's, 80's right up to present day. Undoubtedly we have overlooked some excellent work and apologize for such oversights but it was impossible for us to review all the work produced over the last 40 years. That said, what is presented is representative of the excellent work produced within our industry by some very talented people. We encourage others who choose to expand upon our efforts in future publications to be more inclusive.—***R.P.***

Creativity

According to a famous copywriter, "Copy is the business of advertising." Of course, David Ogilvy meant *print* advertising, admitting that TV was not his chosen medium. Until recently, print was also *our* chosen medium. In fact, our only medium. The illustrations in this book have been selected for their "creativity." What made them creative? How do they differ from the creativity of consumer campaigns?

Creativity is born from knowledge. Knowledge of our market, knowledge of the competition, product knowledge. That's basic. Then comes the giant leap! To translate this knowledge into vivid terms that will hold the viewer's attention. This leads us to positioning: a deliberate choice to stress certain product features, while omitting or subordinating others. And it leads the creative team to search for the unexpected, for a "twist," or an analogy, be it verbal or visual. To quote that other giant of modern advertising, Bill Bernbach, "You can't bore the customer into buying your product!"

It's hard to imagine now, but copy and art did not always work as a team. They proceeded on separate tracks, and art began where copy left off. As one veteran copywriter described it, his copy fell into a deep, dark hole; he only saw it again when it came back "illustrated" and laid out by an art director. It was Bernbach's agency that pioneered the concept of the copy-art team, later adopted with brilliant results by Sudler & Hennessey and other medical agencies.—*J.K.*

Copy Writers

They come from all disciplines—English literature to pharmaceuticals, journalism to pre-med. But first of all they must be good writers, and that talent can be nourished and encouraged but never taught.

The art of writing medical advertising requires knowledge about the product and the science behind it as well as the ability to give life to the data that renders an argument for the product both compelling and luminous, with words that are fresh and memorable.

The art of writing medical advertising is especially difficult, given the medium. Unlike consumer advertising where you might be writing the only ad for a fountain pen in a magazine carrying ads for perfumes, cars, food, and clothes, in medical advertising we are often writing an ad for an antihypertensive to appear in a cardiology book in which most of the ads are for antihypertensives.

So how does a writer make an ad stand out in such circumstances? The good writer goes in search of a product's quiddity, that which gives it distinctness. Then he seeks to capture that uniqueness in words and phrases that bring it to life, that strike a resonant chord in the reader, that illuminate. The best writing makes the reader say, "Yes, that's it." The product is validated (and the sale is made) because the truth, the reality of the product, comes off the page and into the reader's imagination.—*F.H.*

Art Directors

A good art director is subversive. He takes the expected image and twists it into something unexpected and in doing so, makes it unforgettable and part of our visual vocabulary. Anything less is mere decoration. But the image need not be bizarre or eccentric to provoke us or jar us. Instead of an asthmatic child on an examining table, the art director might show us the child with a tear on his cheek staring wistfully out the window, showing how a disease can affect a life.

Because art directors do not think linearly, they are not bound by the same rigors of logic as the rest of us. An image can tell a story as well as words and often does so more tellingly, more inventively, more forcefully.

The other obligation of an art director is design—the way a communication is placed on a page, the type chosen, the way space is divided between image and text. All the elements of design contribute to the power and recall of an ad. Attention to the smallest details of design is the hallmark of great art direction.—*F.H.*

Account Management

The account executive is the linchpin between the client and the agency. He must have a unique combination of knowledge about marketing, sales, advertising, research and production to be effective. The account team is charged with representing the agency both creatively and strategically. This means they have many masters ... not an enviable position. Usually a "great" account person is a strong advocate of the creative product. Without such a love and passion for the creative work, the account person earns the derisive title of "suit" or worse "empty suit." The account team is not only charged with selling the agency's product but the important task of growing the agency's business. Finally, the account service department is the face of the agency and therefore must be both intellectually sound and have a passion for advertising.—*R.P.*

Branding

Clients make products that do something. Advertising agencies turn products into brands. The process of branding creates a personality for the product that turns into an enduring image. Brands are the sum of the emotional feelings a customer has about a product. Branding is all about trust ... customers trust the quality, they trust the value because they trust the image. Customers trust that a brand says something about them that they want said about themselves. In today's complicated world of besotted advertising it is ever more difficult to create a brand. In fact, it takes a fully integrated communications approach to achieve an enduring brand. Notwithstanding the need for a total-communication approach, the advertising agency remains the safekeeper of the brand as it is the agency that, year in and out, makes the images that sustain the brand personality.—**R.P.**

The Client

"A great ad needs a great client."

Good advertising challenges our preconceptions with new words, new images, and new ways of looking at the world.

Good clients know this and are not scared off by the unfamiliar, the unsafe. If communications don't challenge received opinion, there is little hope of changing buying (or, in our case, prescribing) habits.

A client who is convinced of the necessity of advertising, a client who expects tangible results from his advertising, a client who is proud of his advertising—that client will inspire his agency to superior performance.

Fortunately, our industry has had plenty of great clients, as the ads in this volume demonstrate.

The work in *Medicine Avenue* is the result, therefore, of collaborative efforts to which client and agency have contributed.

Together with our clients, we have captured the imagination of physicians and turned a nascent industry into one of the most successful businesses in the world today.—*F.H./J.K.*

The advertisements presented in *Medicine Avenue* are the result of effective collaboration among art, copy and account teams. Sometimes the collaboration can be difficult, even heated. But when the final result is breakthrough advertising that contains a big idea it is all worthwhile. In fact, it is this moment that makes all of us love the business of advertising. The following pages contain some of those moments. We hope you enjoy them as much as we do.—*R.P.*

MEDICINE AVE.

The Story of Medical Advertising in America

Information is fundamental to pharmaceuticals. Prescription products are inexorably linked to envelopes of information describing the conditions they alleviate, instructing on how and when they should be administered, and warning of precautions to be taken in their use.

Because this information is so crucial, the scientific validity of the product messages, who receives them, and how they are delivered take on heightened significance. Issues regarding the public good are ultimately resolved by the interaction of medicine, industry, government, academia, the press, and the public. In the past 100 years, the role and character of medical advertising in the United States has been the subject of an ongoing debate among these parties. The history of medical advertising agencies—the subset of general advertising that for more than 75 years has specialized in promotional programs to professional audiences on prescription drugs—traces the movement of attitudes about communications on healthcare products.

Nothing illustrates this process more clearly than the decision made by organized medicine and pharmaceutical companies in 1905 that determined the character of advertising to physicians for most of the twentieth century. Underlying the pivotal event of 1905 was the competition between "patent medicines" and "ethical drugs." Patent medicines, or "nostrums," had secret formulas and registered tradenames; the scientifically oriented "ethical" revealed their ingredients. During the late 1800's, these two classes of drugs existed on an equal footing. The manufacturers of both classes advertised to physicians and also employed sales staffs to call on doctors and pharmacists. However, patent medicines also advertised heavily to the public.

The American Medical Association was opposed to nostrums. AMA opposition was based in part on the patent medicine companies' practice of attacking the medical profession as a commercial conspiracy and touting their products as a substitute for medical care. But, in the early 1900's American medicine was not well organized and the education of doctors was uneven, so the AMA made little headway in its campaign against patent medicines. Physicians, in fact, were part of the problem. The poorly educated doctors of the day had contributed to the patent medicine boom in the late nineteenth century by prescribing them in great quantities for their patients.

By 1905, however, with an assist from the muckraking journalists of the period who revealed the deceit and real dangers of patent medicines, the AMA began to make progress. The AMA Council on Pharmacy and Chemistry was established that year and began setting standards for drugs. The council's publication *New and Non-Official Remedies* soon became the Bible on drugs for physicians, and medical publications like *The Journal of the American Medical Association* (*JAMA*) used it in deciding whether to accept advertising on a product.

Paul Starr, in his scholarly study *The Social Transformation of American Medicine*, describes the new standards:

> To have a drug accepted, a company had to comply with the AMA council's rules. Not only were drugs forbidden whose manufacturers made false advertising claims or refused to disclose their drug's composition, the council also would not approve any drug that was directly advertised to the public or whose "label, package, or circular" listed the diseases for which the drug was used. Companies would have a choice of markets: If they wished to advertise a drug to doctors they could not advertise it to the public or instruct laymen in its use.[1]

The core qualities of advertising drugs—message, media, and audience—had been restructured to hobble the marketing of patent medicines (soon to be further restricted by the establishment of the Food and Drug Administration through the Pure Food and Drug Act of 1906, which created regulatory authority in the field). This restructuring also enhanced the authority of physicians to control the more potent and more effective pharmaceutical armamentarium that was emerging from advances in biology and chemistry.

Faced with the choice put to them by the AMA, which for many years issued a seal of approval on pharmaceuticals, companies like Lilly, Upjohn, Wyeth and Parke-Davis, chose the "ethical" route and, based on a decision on advertising policy, the character of the pharmaceutical industry as we know it today was established. The scientifically directed companies instructed their advertising agencies or internal ad departments to conform to the AMA standards and by so doing, these agencies and departments became the forerunners of the medical advertising specialization.

HARRY PHIBBS AND THE AMA

The first purely medical advertising agency appears to have been founded in Chicago by Harry C. Phibbs in 1921. Phibbs had emigrated from Ireland to the U.S. via Canada. He was a multi-talented man, having been an actor, artist, newspaper photographer and salesman for the drug firm Burroughs Wellcome where he advanced to middle management. He was working at an advertising agency in Chicago when, according to the family legend, he was approached by his friend Dr. Morris Fishbein (later a powerful force at the American Medical Association, but then in an editorial position on *JAMA*) who suggested he go out on his own targeting ethical drug accounts. Fishbein told Phibbs, according to son Roderick Phibbs, that the AMA would open doors for him because they were looking for an agency to provide "respectable scientific" advertising for their publications. Phibbs started out with $200 working capital and his wife as his secretary/assistant. One of the first accounts of Harry C. Phibbs Advertising Co. was his former employer, Burroughs Wellcome.

Other family members confirm that it was acknowledged fact at the Phibbs agency that "the AMA put Harry in business." To anyone familiar with Morris Fishbein's career—he was an energetic, self-confident activist of strong opinions—the idea that Fishbein could have helped Phibbs, a friend, by referring clients to him is extremely plausible. Phibbs and Fishbein remained close over the years. In a 1958 note to Fishbein from Phibbs, retained in the Fishbein archive at the University of Chicago, Phibbs notes their common membership in the "old pioneers party" and refers to their long association.[2] Fishbein was on the front line in the AMA offensive in the 1920's against patent medicines and quackery. In an August 19, 1926, article in *Printers' Ink*, he displays attitudes consistent with his taking steps to encourage ethically oriented advertising. He wrote:

This is why he (the physician) has been so unyielding in his fight on the quack, the cure-all, and the highly commercialized "remedies" that have abused advertising in their effort to reach the people. Because advertising has been the means through which these abuses have been put over, it was inevitable that the ethical physician should look with suspicion upon it as a force connected even remotely with medicine and be more or less prejudiced in his viewpoint.

Fortunately, though, many leading advertisers and advertising agencies are already aware of the fact that the sale of commodities on the basis of scientific evidence will demand evidence that is established, and logic that is logical ...

In the preparation of such copy, advertising writers have naturally been compelled to consult vast amounts of controversial medical literature leading up to the opinion held today, and then to submit the copy to recognized authorities, with a view to checking all of the claims made. It is this cooperation between modern advertising and modern organized medicine that will yield the best results for the public good.[3]

The Phibbs agency worked for major pharmaceutical firms for over 50 years. Harry Phibbs died in 1960. The company was sold to Frank J. Corbett in 1970.

Chicago was the birthplace of another landmark medical agency. William Douglas McAdams, whose background was journalism and public relations, founded his agency there in 1926. In the beginning, McAdams was a general "package goods" agency with such accounts as Van Camps Beans and Mother's Oats. The link to the agency's eventual medical specialization was business from E.R. Squibb—advertising for cod liver oil.

Rx Advertising Misses the Madison Avenue Boom

McAdams moved its operations to New York City in the 1930's, continuing with Squibb but also pursuing nonmedical accounts. In 1939, the decision was made to concentrate only on professional advertising to physicians. This decision expressed a faith in the future growth of medical advertising, for pharmaceutical promotion prior to World War II was a backwater compared to the boom that general advertising was experiencing. Buoyed by the expansionist 1920's and not markedly impaired by the depression years of the early 1930's, consumer advertising had soared. The combination of a plethora of heavily advertised consumer products (automobiles, household appliances, soaps, foods, cosmetics, and cigarettes) with effective media (color enhanced magazines, radio, outdoor, and newspapers) and fueled by a mass-marketing philosophy, created the giant Madison Avenue advertising agencies and hundreds of lucrative smaller shops around the country. In contrast, pharmaceutical promotion was an unglamorous trade exercise that stressed salesperson rapport and service to physicians and pharmacists. There was little product differentiation since the companies were, for the most part, marketing generic drugs.

Journal advertising in a limited number of publications—*JAMA*, *Medical Economics*, *Modern Medicine* and a few state journals—was used for the few branded products and companies who did invest in institutional advertising. (Squibb was successful with a campaign that associated the company with a medical sage of Baghdad who pronounced that "quality is the priceless ingredient" and that it rested on the honesty and integrity of the manufacturer.) In the 1930's, substantial advertising budgets did exist for "ethical OTC," branded non-Rx products that companies promoted to MDs and pharmacists, relying on sales from professional recommendation.

These budgets, however, were the province of the manufacturer's advertising department, which often had its own creative staff, and in a way competed with agencies for the limited funds available. Given sizable "in-house" operations, it is understandable that a number of founders of early medical agencies started their careers at these companies. A notable example is the presence of Arthur E. Sudler and Matthew J. Hennessey at the advertising department of E.R. Squibb in 1934 when Hennessey joined the company. In describing the nature of the work, Hennessey recalls, "In those days, the major emphasis was on what Squibb referred to as "home necessities"—Squibb Cod Liver Oil, Dental Cream, Milk of Magnesia, etc. The pharmaceutical specialties were not promoted then except through the detail force. Most of our activities were designing window displays, in-store materials and sales promotion for the sales force."[4] Although professional advertising was secondary, enough promotional business existed for Sudler to leave Squibb in 1936 to set up an art studio. Hennessey joined him and Squibb was one of their first clients.

Another legendary name in medical advertising began on the company side. Dr. Arthur M. Sackler, after earning his medical degree from New York University,

ARTHUR E. SUDLER (1905—1968)

As a young man, Arthur Sudler aspired to be a fine arts painter. He attended art school studying under such famous teachers as John Sloan and Robert Henri. But his career collided with the Great Depression and he went to work in the promotion department of Squibb, where he advanced to creative director. In 1936, he set up his own art studio with Squibb as his first client.

Although he continued to paint, Sudler's artistic drive was now expressed through the work of his studio. When the boom in prescription drugs arrived after World War II, Sudler & Hennessey, given the Squibb experience, was ideally positioned to catch the wave, evolving into a full service advertising agency in 1953. However, Sudler did more than go with the flow; he established its direction. His knowledge of art, his taste and his respect for talent produced a remarkably productive creative environment. He hired outstanding designers, developed others into creative stars, and bought the work of notable artists for use in pharmaceutical campaigns.

S&H became a mecca for those dedicated to creative excellence with such notable designers on staff as Herb Lubalin, Ernie Smith, George Lois, Dick Jones, Arthur Ludwig, Helmut Krone and Sam Scali. Sudler set a high standard—the integration of art and copy, and reader involvement achieved through provocative, impactful graphics. His talent was the basis for "the pharmaceutical look," —a style which was followed by a generation of writers and designers and is still with us today.

worked as advertising manager for Schering. He was to go on to a vastly successful and influential career with the McAdams agency. While at Schering, Sackler used the services of a young German type designer/salesman, L.W. Frohlich, who had come to this country in 1931. A close friendship developed. Frohlich later founded a landmark medical agency and over the years continued his association with Sackler in numerous business ventures. Frohlich, Hennessey, Sackler, Sudler all were to leave their mark on medical advertising and all served an apprenticeship at or through company advertising units in the 1930's.

ARTHUR M. SACKLER, M.D. (1913—1987)

No single individual did more to shape the character of medical advertising than the multi-talented Dr. Arthur Sackler. His seminal contribution was bringing the full power of advertising and promotion to pharmaceutical marketing. Until the early 1950's, "ethical drug" promotion had been a low-key "trade" exercise relying principally on sales calls to physicians. The campaign conducted by Sackler's agency, William Douglas McAdams, for the antibiotic Terramycin (Pfizer) forever changed the Rx industry's marketing model. He showed how intelligently written, strikingly illustrated/designed advertising used in volume could greatly influence the success of a product.

No area of healthcare communications remained untouched by Sackler's restless ingenuity—advertising, publishing, market research, public relations, medical education, closed circuit television and consumer advertising of Rx products.

As the founder of the tabloid Medical Tribune he further affirmed his belief in medical communications as a positive force for scientific advancement. He will also be remembered as a connoisseur of the arts—his Far Eastern collection was world-renowned—and for his extensive philanthropy to museums, universities and medical institutions, both here and abroad.

THE ADVERTISEMENTS ...

. . . in *Medicine Avenue* are interspersed throughout the text so as
to be representative of the historical period being described. They
were selected for their creative excellence and also to illustrate
themes typical of medical advertising—for example, the depiction
of symptoms, scientific explanation of drug mechanisms, and the
patient's positive response to medication.

Our selection was limited to available material and so, as
was noted previously, we may have inadvertently neglected
worthy work. We believe the advertising included speaks to the
writing and design skill displayed by our industry over the
years—talent, of which we in medical advertising can be proud.

AGENCY NAMES

Over the years the names of medical advertising agencies have
changed with mergers, new principals rising from the ranks,
and acquisitions by consumer agencies. *Medicine Avenue* has not
attempted to trace this shifting nomenclature. The transience of names
presents too complex a historical process and, in our opinion, is
incidental to the overall story of medical advertising in America. Where
a name change represents a turning point, it is noted, but for the most
part, we have stayed with the foundation names of agencies, dropping
secondary elements for brevity.

For example, William Douglas McAdams, after first mention is
shortened to McAdams. L.W. Frohlich/Intercon becomes Frohlich.
This editing not only speeds up the text but is true to the language
of the industry where abbreviated names—Sudler, Torre, Rosenthal,
Lally, Ferguson, etc.—are part of the working vocabulary.

The Boom Years

Immediately after WWII the pace of medical advertising intensified. Research provided breakthrough products; Medicine Avenue provided a new promotional philosophy and a new promotional style, launching the industry's "Golden Age."

THE FOUNDERS OF MEDICINE AVENUE

Moving into the 1940's, Frohlich, Hennessey, Sackler and Sudler were to establish agencies that would become central to medical advertising for the next 20 years. In 1942, Hennessey became a partner with Sudler in Sudler & Hennessey, at that time a design studio. Also in 1942, Sackler bought into William Douglas McAdams, on his way to controlling ownership of the agency. In 1943, Frohlich opened his agency. The 1940's saw another important name enter the agency lexicon—Paul Klemtner, who had served Rx clients as a certified public accountant in the late 1930's. In addition to auditing and financial advice, he counseled his clients to increase their promotional activities—principally detailing—and to focus on prescribing rather than dispensing MDs. He eventually set up an agency in Newark, NJ, in 1942 to execute the programs he had championed.

Coming out of World War II, there existed a core of medically oriented agencies—Frohlich, Klemtner, McAdams, Phibbs, Sudler & Hennessey and Murray Breese, a New York shop that offered competition to McAdams prior to the war and continued on the scene into the 1940's. The business of pharmaceutical advertising was

1

2

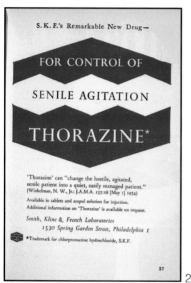

3

growing rapidly with the advent of new products. For example, Premarin (Wyeth-Ayerst) had been introduced in 1941 and during the war medical advances made in antibiotics and steroids were harbingers of what was to come. In Chicago, Jordan Sieber (1949) opened, and in New York, the husband and wife team of Noyes & Sproul went into business with A.H. Robins as their key account. Also, the colorful Dr. Cortez F. Enloe, a physician and former Air Force colonel, founded his agency, gaining business from Squibb which, as a major spender, nurtured a number of the early agencies. Consumer agencies, like Doherty, Clifford, Steers & Shenfield, which handled business for Merck, recognized a new market for promotion services and began to compete with the specialized agencies.

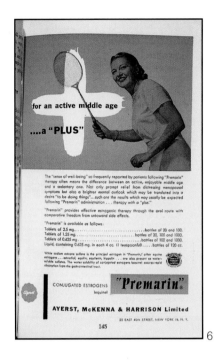

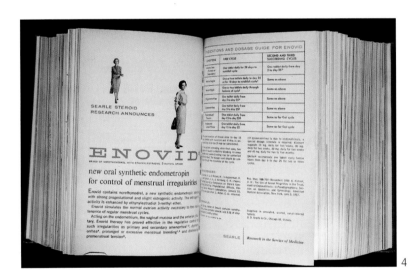

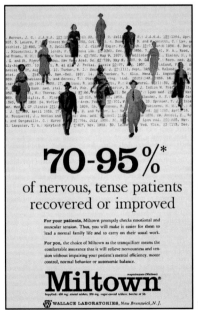

1 *CLIENT:* Merck (1950). 2 *CLIENT:* Smith, Kline & French (1954). 3 *CLIENT:* Upjohn.
AGENCY: McAdams (the first oral antidiabetic drug, 1957). 4 *CLIENT:* Searle. *AGENCY:* R. E. Wilson.
COPY: Dick Grossman (note the indication for The Pill: 'to control menstrual irregularity'! 1957).
5 *CLIENT:* Pfizer. *AGENCY:* McAdams (the first teaser ad in our industry, prior to the introduction of Terramycin. 1949). 6 *CLIENT:* Ayerst, McKenna & Harrison (1947). 7 *CLIENT:* Wallace.
AGENCY: Ted Bates (1950).

THE "WONDER DRUG" WAVE

This group of agencies was ideally positioned to benefit from the flood of new pharmaceuticals that emerged from European and American research laboratories in the 1950's. The "wonder drug" era had arrived. Diseases previously untreatable suddenly could be cured or alleviated by new medication. Antibiotics, steroids, antihistamines, oral hypoglycemic, psychotropics and anti-hypertensives revolutionized medical practice. Wall Street, Washington, American medicine, the pharmaceutical industry, and the medical advertising agencies shared in the triumph of new chemical and biological discoveries that significantly improved public health and the quality of living. Medical advertising agencies had the enviable task of delivering the inspiring message of technological advances to healthcare practitioners.

1

Not surprisingly, medical advertising reflected this technological revolution and went through a comparable transformation. Funded by sizable budgets, agencies began to draw upon the creative talent of Madison Avenue and abandon the catalogue look of trade advertising. Impactful graphics, challenging copy, and saturation media strategies were introduced for journal ads, direct mail, sampling units, convention exhibits and sales aids. Most of the basic promotional techniques of Rx promotion took shape at this time. If a watershed event in this transition can be identified, it is probably the intensive campaign McAdams conducted, led by Dr. Sackler, for Terramycin (Pfizer) and the appearance in 1952 of the Pfizer house organ *Spectrum* as a multi-page insert in *JAMA* to build the company's status and as an advertising vehicle.

2

3

1 *CLIENT:* Pfizer. *AGENCY:* McAdams.
ARTIST: Ben Shahn (1952).
2 *CLIENT:* Upjohn. *AD:* Lester Beall (1948).
3 *CLIENT:* Upjohn. *AD:* Will Burtin (1948).

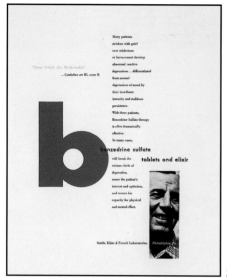

1 *CLIENT:* Abbott. *AD:* Lester Beall (1941).
2 *CLIENT:* Smith, Kline & French.
AD: Lester Beall (1943). 3 *CLIENT:* Upjohn.
AGENCY: McAdams. *AD:* Will Burtin (1950).
4 *CLIENT:* Pfizer. *AGENCY:* McAdams.
AD: Harry Zelenko. *COPY:* John Kallir (1952).
5 *CLIENT:* Upjohn. *AGENCY:* McAdams.
AD: Rudy Wolff. (1950s). 6 *CLIENT:* Schering.
AGENCY: L. W.Frohlich. *AD:* Ken Lavey.
ILLUSTR: Eric Carle (1950s). 7 *CLIENT:* United Fruit.
AGENCY: McAdams. *AD:* Dave Epstein.
ILLUSTR.: Fred Witzig (1950s).

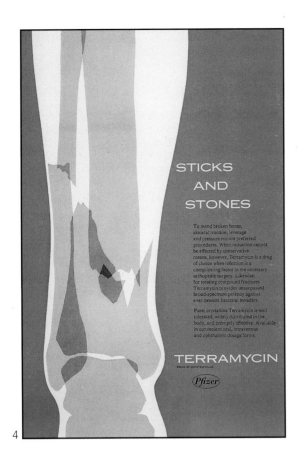

STICKS
AND
STONES

To mend broken bones,
skeletal traction, leverage
and pressure remain preferred
procedures. When reduction cannot
be effected by conservative
means, however, Terramycin is a drug
of choice when infection is a
complicating factor in the necessary
orthopedic surgery. Likewise,
for treating compound fractures
Terramycin provides unsurpassed
broad-spectrum potency against
ever-present bacterial invaders.

Pure, crystalline Terramycin is well
tolerated, widely distributed in the
body, and promptly effective. Available
in convenient oral, intravenous
and ophthalmic dosage forms.

TERRAMYCIN
BRAND OF OXYTETRACYCLINE
Pfizer

4

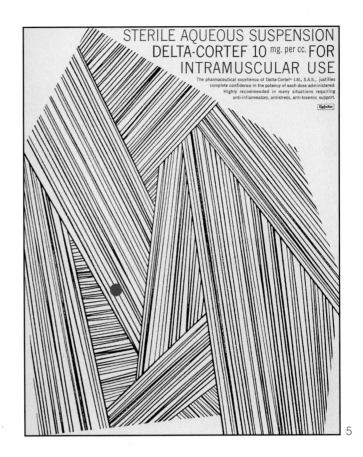

STERILE AQUEOUS SUSPENSION
DELTA-CORTEF 10 mg. per cc. FOR
INTRAMUSCULAR USE

The pharmaceutical excellence of Delta-Cortef® I.M., S.A.S., justifies
complete confidence in the potency of each dose administered.
Highly recommended in many situations requiring
anti-inflammatory, antistress, anti-toxemic support.

Upjohn

5

when yesterday's indulgence
becomes today's allergy
Chlor-Trimeton Repetabs 8 or 12 mg.

6

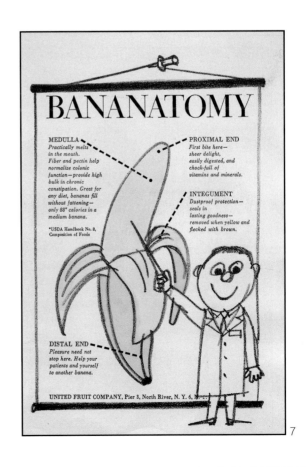

BANANATOMY

MEDULLA
Practically melts
in the mouth.
Fiber and pectin help
normalize colonic
function—provide high
bulk in chronic
constipation. Great for
any diet, bananas fill
without fattening—
only 88* calories in a
medium banana.

*USDA Handbook No. 8,
Composition of Foods

PROXIMAL END
First bite here—
sheer delight,
easily digested, and
chock-full of
vitamins and minerals.

INTEGUMENT
Dustproof protection—
seals in
lasting goodness—
removed when yellow and
flecked with brown.

DISTAL END
Pleasure need not
stop here. Help your
patients and yourself
to another banana.

UNITED FRUIT COMPANY, Pier 3, North River, N. Y. 6,

7

At this time, company field forces were small, numbering in the hundreds rather than the thousands as they do today. Accordingly, to reach physicians, a heavy promotional role was given to non-personal selling techniques—direct mail of all kinds and journal advertising. "During this period," Hennessey recalls, "it was difficult for anyone in the communications business to miss. The drug industry became alive with [new products] and the need to spread the good news."[5] Cortez Enloe, at a seminar on pharmaceutical marketing in 1955, commented, "In 1946, there were four or five genuine medical advertising agencies in the pharmaceutical business. Today, there are eighteen ... that also indicates that a lot of money is being spent by advertising agencies, few of which have gone broke ..."[6] Medical advertising was booming along with the pharmaceutical industry.

The boom stimulated the founding of new Rx agencies. Robert E. Wilson, after working in the advertising departments of G.D. Searle and William R. Warner, went out on his own to open his agency in New York in 1952. In Philadelphia, in proximity to a concentration of Rx manufacturers, Ted Thomas began business in 1953 in competition with Lee Ramsdell and the consumer agency Lewis & Gillman, which handled advertising for American Home Products' ethical drug company Wyeth. Jordan Sieber in Chicago became Jordan Sieber

CLIENT: Merrell.
AGENCY: Sudler & Hennessey.
AD: Herb Lubalin.
COPY: Don Clark. (1954).

Corbett in 1955 when Frank J. Corbett, after working for manufacturers in the East and in California, moved to the agency side of the business. Consumer agencies attracted to the pharmaceutical business in the mid-1950's were Benton & Bowles, Charles W. Hoyt (Merck), Fuller & Smith & Ross (Lilly), Doremus-Eshleman (SKF), Ruthruff & Ryan (Lederle), and BBDO (Merck).

A shortage of knowledgeable copywriters, art directors, research and account personnel allowed for a concentration of industry billing at the older agencies, particularly McAdams and Frohlich. These two agencies, never truly rivals based on the friendship of Dr. Sackler and Frohlich, were in a dominant position. With "ethical drug" expertise in such demand and with relationships with their clients so strong, each was able to handle competitive products with no objection from the manufacturers. For example, Frohlich began working for two directly competitive antihistamines in 1949—Chlor-Trimeton (Schering) and Benadryl (Parke-Davis)—and successfully maintained this arrangement into the 1960's.

NEW AGENCIES EMERGE

As product lines grew and the sales stakes mounted, the business being generated by the burgeoning pharmaceutical industry overran the older and newly founded agencies. The inevitable proliferation of additional agencies began drawing on the talent pool that had been maturing at companies and at the older agencies. In New York, a dramatic event set an example for others to follow—the formation of Burdick, Becker and Fitzsimmons in 1957. Becker had been an ad manager at Squibb; Fitzsimmons came from the Chicago Rx scene; but the significant defection from the older agencies was Dean Burdick who had been one of the top executives at McAdams. Although the three-way partnership lasted only a year, with Fitzsimmons leaving to set up his own agency, a pattern had been established. The "ground floor" agencies would become training grounds for new agencies which, in turn, would train a new crop of competitors in what had become a sizable, well-funded advertising specialty. John Kallir left McAdams and with Warren Ross and Jerry Philips, who had also been at McAdams, founded Kallir Philips Ross in 1962, the same year Frank Corbett

1

2

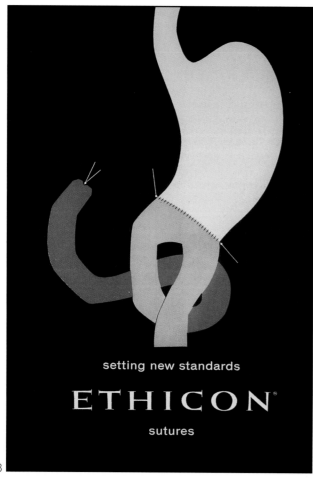

3

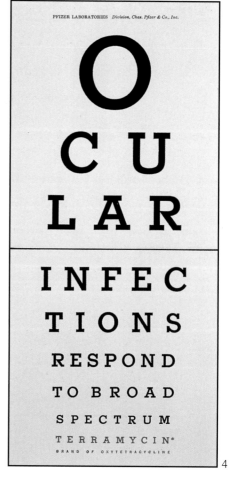

4

resigned from JSC. The demand for experienced Rx advertising talent soon had him in business for himself.

The character of pharmaceutical promotion had markedly changed in intensity and style. Competition among manufacturers as they introduced dozens of new brand names during the 1950's expressed itself in great quantities of direct mail, medical journals bulked up by multi-page, four-color ads and heavy stock inserts, elaborate exhibits at medical conventions, widespread sampling and increased MD calls by sales representatives. At a 1959 seminar of pharmaceutical marketing, Tobias Wagner, director of advertising at SmithKline & French, had this to say about direct mail: "Perhaps the biggest problem inherent in pharmaceutical promotion is the sheer bulk of direct mail received by the physician. Last year, (1958) according to one reliable source, there was a slight decrease in total mailings: 3902 (comprising 6,513 pieces) in 1957. But the volume is still formidable." He also noted, "... direct mail is the physician's favorite whipping boy; he habitually brands it as inordinately expensive and as a chief factor contributing to the high cost of drugs ..."[7]

LUDWIG WILHELM FROHLICH (1913-1971)

L.W. Frohlich was a combination of esthetic sensibilities and business acumen. His superb taste was evidenced by the fashion statement of his finely tailored suits, the furnishings and art in his New York townhouse, and the high standard he set for the graphics in the work his advertising agency produced.

He arrived in this country in 1931 as a representative for a German type company. His talents came to the attention of the Schering advertising manager, Dr. Arthur Sackler, who encouraged him to go into business for himself. Frohlich set up an art studio in 1939, and in 1944 it was incorporated as an advertising agency. Over the years a number of art directors who achieved recognition in consumer advertising served an apprenticeship at LWF.

On the business side, he was a visionary. L.W. Frohlich/Intercon was operating internationally in European markets and in Japan well in advance of its competitors. As a major partner in the formation of the market-auditing firm IMS, Frohlich displayed his capacity to recognize the long-term, informational needs of the pharmaceutical industry. His vision of a global market for advertising and research services survived his untimely death in his late 50s

1 *CLIENT:* Upjohn. *AGENCY:*McAdams. *AD:* Rudy Wolff. *ILLUSTR.:* R.O. Blechman (1950s). 2 *CLIENT:* Upjohn. *AGENCY:* McAdams.*AD:* Rudy Wolff. *ILLUSTR.:* Andy Warhol (1950s). 3 *CLIENT:* Ethicon. *AGENCY:* L. W. Frohlich. *AD:* Ken Lavey (1950s). 4 *CLIENT:* Pfizer. *AGENCY:* McAdams. *AD:* Harry Zelenko. *COPY:* John Kallir (1952).

1 *CLIENT:* Warner-Chilcott. *AGENCY:* Sudler
& Hennessey. *AD:* Herb Lubalin (1950s).
2 *CLIENT:* A. H. Robins. *AGENCY:* Sudler &
Hennessey. *AD:* Ernie Smith. (1954).
3 *CLIENT:* Schering. *AGENCY:* Sudler &
Hennessey. *AD:* Herb Lubalin.
PHOTOG.: Carl Fischer (1956).

In-House Advertising Departments

While the emphasis of this brief historic survey is on the work of specialized agencies, important contributions have been made also in the advertising departments of pharmaceutical companies—sometimes in collaboration with an agency, at other times entirely "in house." Every major company employed copywriters and at least one art director in its advertising department. Thus, E.R. Squibb honed the talents of Arthur E. Sudler, Matthew J. Hennessey, Robert A. Becker and Dr. Felix Marti Ibanez, the future founder of *MD* magazine, while Schering's advertising department launched the career of Dr. Arthur M. Sackler.

Outstanding examples of internal agency operations are the two Swiss companies CIBA and Geigy. In the postwar years the American subsidiary of CIBA was headed by Paul Erni, a brother of the well known Swiss artist Hans Erni. Aware of new trends in the graphic arts, CIBA commissioned James Fogelman to create its corporate image, including company logo, packaging and letterhead, as well as advertising. For a number of years, CIBA provided, as educational materials, the work of the talented illustrators Frank Netter and Paul Peck in the *CIBA Symposium* series. Geigy, too, only rarely turned to outside help. Under the direction of Bob Baldini (later to become president of Key Pharmaceuticals), Geigy staffed its in-house agency with a brilliant group of writers and art directors. The company's worldwide advertising was stylized by the noted designer Gottfried Henecker.

Equally autonomous were the advertising departments of Smith Kline & French and Abbott Laboratories under its advertising manager William Pratt. At Abbott, Charles S. Downs developed the publication *What's New*, which was distributed to physicians as an element in the company's promotional program. He recruited notable authors and artists as contributors—such famous names as Carl Sandburg, William Saroyan, Ben Shahn and Thomas Hart Benton. Other widely distributed house organs were Upjohn's *Scope*, Sharp and Dohme's *Seminars*, and Roche's *Image*.

While the Upjohn Company relied heavily on the service of the McAdams agency, some of its most significant innovations originated in Kalamazoo. What had been started by Lester Beall was continued by Will Burtin. Trained in the Bauhaus tradition, Burtin had fled Hitler's Germany in 1938. He became design consultant to Upjohn in 1948, an association that lasted for more than 20 years. His contributions included a new format for professional advertising and two internationally acclaimed exhibits: giant walk-through models of a cell and of the human brain.

Advertising managers and creative directors at companies had a strong influence on the character of medical advertising, particularly in the period 1950 to 1970, prior to the delegation of responsibility for advertising to product management at manufacturers. Some of the people who have left their mark on the industry include: Norman Sprei (Squibb); Rollie Noel (Bristol); Robert Devanna, Irwin Lerner and Ira Contant (Roche); John Hogan, Edward Steel (McNeil); Mal Freeman, Frank Mann (Robins); Bud Nelson, (Ortho, Syntex); Richard Truby, Robert Handy (Upjohn); John Spitznagel (Wyeth); Edward Whitney (Pfizer and W-C); Gene McCabe, Thomas Beckett and George DiDomizio (Merck); William Gulick (Bristol, Roche); Toby Wagner (SKF); Robert Beine and William Pratt (Abbott); Audrey Girard (Roerig); Robert Oppenheimer and Austin Daley (Lederle); Bob Baldini and Charlie Hackett (CIBA-Geigy); Clifford Parish (Burroughs Wellcome); and Whitmore Jensen (Ayerst).—*J.K.*

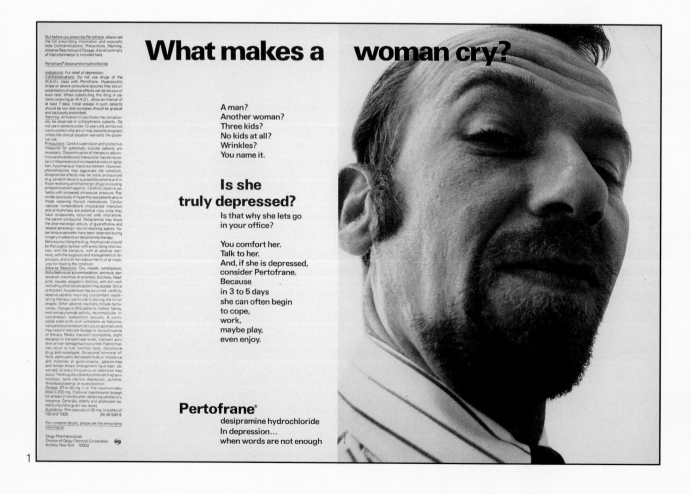

1 *Client:* Geigy. *Agency:* In-house.
AD: Felix Muckenhirn. *Copy:* Ivan Manson.
(1960s). **2** *Client:* Geigy. *Agency:* In-house.
AD: Fred Troller. (1962). **3** *Client:* Smith,
Kline & French. *Agency:* In-house.
AD: Warren Blair, Wm. Schilling.
Illustr.: Brad Holland, Bill Barron (1968).

"I'm at the   **end of my rope."**

Blinded by depression, groping anxiously for meaning in what he sees as a hopeless, precarious existence, the depressed patient is often emotionally pulled in opposite directions. While his depression is immobilizing him with feelings of withdrawal, lack of interest, and fatigue, the accompanying anxiety keeps him awake nights worrying about the future. For these patients, there is no better tricyclic than Tofranil-PM. In a recent study of anxious depressed patients the quality of sleep and rising time was significantly better with imipramine pamoate group than in an amitriptyline [Elavil] treated group. Other measures of relief were not significantly different.

Tofranil-PM
imipramine **pamoate**

Unsurpassed effectiveness among tricyclics in relieving anxiety, sleep disturbances and other symptoms of depression.

1

Copelessness   Tofranil-PM   Geigy
imipramine **pamoate**

Unsurpassed effectiveness among tricyclics in relieving symptoms of depression.

2

1 *CLIENT:* Geigy. *AGENCY:* In-house. *AD:* John deCesare.
ILLUSTR.: Eugène Mihaesco *COPY:* Bill Hackett.
(1960s). 2 *CLIENT:* Geigy. *AGENCY:* In-house.
AD: John deCesare. *ILLUSTR.:* Eugène Mihaesco.
COPY: Bill Hackett (1960s). 3 *CLIENT:* Geigy.
AGENCY: In-house. *AD:* Felix Muckenhirn.
COPY: Ivan Manson. (1960s).

For cold sufferers with aches and pains...

'Ornex' does double duty

'Ornex' capsules contain both an analgesic and a decongestant.

Acetaminophen, the effective analgesic in 'Ornex', gives cold sufferers the relief they want from headaches, aches, pains and fever.

Phenylpropanolamine, the dependable decongestant, relieves upper respiratory congestion.

Analgesic *and* decongestant.

That's the 'Ornex' approach.

And the big difference.

The 'Ornex' formula: Each capsule contains:
Acetaminophen .... 325 mg.
Phenylpropanolamine HCl .... 18 mg.

ORNEX®
DECONGESTANT/ANALGESIC
No Sedatives   No Antihistamines

1

1 *Client:* Smith, Kline & French. *Agency:* In-house.
AD: Alan J. Klawans. *Illustr.:* Ed Koren. (1973).
2 *Client:* Geigy. *Agency:* In-house. *AD:* Fred Troller.
Photog.: Michael Gilligan (1960s).

CLIENT: Ciba-Geigy. AGENCY: C&G Advertising.
AD: Ron Vareltzis. COPY: Nancy Benton (1986).

The 60's

Regulation Reshapes Rx Advertising

The Kefauver hearings resulted in legislation giving the FDA expanded authority over pharmaceutical research and the approval of new drugs. It also empowered the FDA to monitor closely pharmaceutical promotion. After a period of adjustment, manufacturers and ad agencies learned to live within the new environment and, with research still producing milestone products, the boom continued.

BACKLASH TO THE PROMOTIONAL EXPLOSION

The change in Rx promotion did not sit well with some physicians, academics, and consumerists of the day. Since the turn of the century, pharmaceutical and scientifically oriented health products companies—to set themselves apart from the excesses of advertising by quacks and patent medicines—had taken a conservative tone in their promotion, adopting the non-commercial coloration of their customers, physicians and hospitals. The promotion of the 1950's was a sharp break from this quasi-institutional stance. To some, the new style of promotion was offensive and the volume excessive. Moreover, drug prices had increased, reflecting the level of investment in research and the market value of therapeutic improvement provided by the new products. But some saw higher prices taking advantage of patients. And, they viewed climbing stock values and high return-on-investment as evidence of exploitation of the public by the industry.

Additionally, some wonder drugs had run into serious problems. Chloromycetin (Parke-Davis), a widely used antibiotic, was found to cause fatal blood dyscrasias. Negative research findings, it was discovered, had been suppressed on MER-29 (Merrell), an aggressively advertised cholesterol-lowering agent, and the product was withdrawn. A scandal developed over an FDA official accepting income from a drug company for reprints of articles in a publication he edited. Following an FTC investigation, five of the biggest drug companies were indicted for collusion to fix antibiotic prices. A patina of complaint and criticism began to dull the luster of the pharmaceutical industry, and as the industry became a political target, its advertising and promotional practices came in for negative scrutiny.

The social critique of the pharmaceutical industry climaxed at a hearing of the Subcommittee on Antitrust and Monopoly of the Senate's Judiciary Committee chaired by Estes Kefauver of Tennessee. Kefauver had gained national attention through televised hearings he had conducted around the country on organized crime. He had been an unsuccessful vice presidential candidate, running with Adlai Stevenson in 1956. In the late 1950's, he turned his attention to "administered prices," first focusing on the auto, steel and baking industries. These investigations sparked little interest, but when he turned to the drug industry, he struck a sensitive issue with the public and the media on the subject of "prices, profits, and promotion."

On the opening day of the hearing, December 7, 1959, Kefauver, in his prefacing remarks, established the anti-industry stance of the committee's investigation:

It is our purpose to inquire into the question of whether the drug manufacturers are setting their prices at an excessive level ... to determine whether the public is adequately protected by competition and, if not, to devise some means of securing such protection ... the consumer's ability to shop around for lower prices... is severely restricted by the fact that prescriptions are usually written in terms of trade names rather than generic names ... there is... in ethical drugs an intermediary, as there must be, between the producer and the buyer, namely, the physician who writes the prescription. As a consequence, the drug industry is unusual in that he who buys does not order and he who orders does not buy.[8]

Kefauver vs. The Pharmaceutical Industry

The first witness, Francis C. Brown, president of Schering Corporation, was questioned on the company's pricing on its steroid, Meticorten (prednisone). Concentrating only on production costs, Kefauver charged the product was overpriced.

The next morning, working with cost analysis provided by the committee, headlines in newspapers across the country labeled the industry as profiteers. For example:

"Find Drug Markups As High As 7,000 %" (New York Daily News)

"Drug Firm Accused of Boosting Product Price 7,000% Above Cost"

(Los Angeles Times)[9]

Kefauver and his staff had scored a telling publicity victory over the drug industry, which subsequent corrective testimony as to the cost of research, promotion, and distribution by Brown, John T. Connor (Merck), E. Gifford Upjohn (Upjohn) and other drug executives could not reverse. The crusading senator continued the hearings on the drug industry, generating further negative press throughout 1960 and 1961 on company pricing, licensing, research, and opposition to generic drugs. Witnesses from all aspects of the pharmaceutical scene appeared before the committee: numerous Rx company executives, representatives of the AMA and other medical groups, the Pharmaceutical

Manufacturers Association, FDA, voluntary health associations, medical authorities on research, and academic critics of the industry. Many mounted a spirited defense of the industry and its contribution to American medical care, but Kefauver and his staff were able to maintain a steady drumbeat of provocative charges and fault-finding.

In early 1962, the committee turned its attention to medical advertising agencies, having subpoenaed files from the McAdams and Frohlich agencies. By then, legislation to give FDA greater authority over Rx advertising had been proposed. Kefauver, in opening the hearing on January 30, 1962, into medical advertising, said, "... a doctor who is misled by excessive claims may unwittingly prescribe the wrong drug for his patient. The evidence already presented before our sub-committee reveals that great skill goes into the devising of words and phrases which in advertisements have great significance to the physician."[10] In short, the political attack on the industry held that physicians were being unduly influenced by promotion for the commercial gain of advertisers and to the detriment of the public's health.

In five days of hearings, Kefauver and his staff challenged representatives of McAdams and Frohlich to defend their work. It was charged that promotional consideration, rather than science, had influenced the content of individual ads and mailers (headlines, graphics, and body text were dealt with in detail), and that commercial intent was visible in internal memos and correspondence on such matters as copy clearance with *JAMA* and the holding of medical symposia.

In the two and one-half years of the hearings, a litany of complaints about the pharmaceutical industry had been put on the record. The hearing's transcript would be mined by industry critics for decades. However, legislation to change drug regulation—the Kefauver-Harris Amendments to the 1938 Food, Drug and Cosmetic Act—was encountering substantial opposition in Congress, especially proposals on patents and compulsory licensing.

Thalidomide and Kefauver Legislation

Then, history repeated itself to give Washington greater control over prescription drugs. The Pure Food and Drug Act of 1906, which established the FDA, had received powerful stimulus from Upton Sinclair's novel *The Jungle*, which exposed the unhealthy conditions of the meat packing industry. Similarly, the sulfanilamide syrup tragedy in 1938 in which almost 100 children died due to an untested ingredient influenced Congress to pass the Food, Drug and Cosmetic Act which gave FDA authority over product safety. In 1962, the event that affected Congress and salvaged the Kefauver legislation was the thalidomide disaster.

A sedative developed by a small German manufacturer had been widely sold overseas since 1957, but had not been approved for marketing in the U.S. When it was discovered that thousands of European children had been born with deformed limbs because their pregnant mothers had taken the drug, a wave of revulsion and concern about drugs swept the world. Opposition to increasing the powers of the FDA—the agency that had fortuitously prevented the product from being used in the United States—evaporated, and in the face of this drug-induced calamity, the Kefauver-Harris Amendments passed 78 to 0 in the Senate and 347 to 0 in the House of Representatives.

The Kefauver-Harris Amendments greatly extended FDA's oversight of pharmaceutical advertising, giving the regulatory agency responsibility to judge the truthfulness and scientific accuracy of promotional messages, and also requiring advertisers to provide information on side effects, precautions, and contraindications in conjunction with product claims. A "fair balance" presentation was required—effectiveness contrasted to precautionary information—and to emphatically achieve this end, advertisements had also to include a "brief summary" of the product's package insert. The regulatory mechanics FDA imposed to achieve "fair balance" and "brief summary" markedly altered Rx advertising in the 1960's and continue to determine its content today.

New Regulations Over Pharmaceutical Advertising

The power to decide on regulations governing prescription drug advertising had been delegated to the FDA and the agency issued rules which, at first, appeared unworkable to the industry. The complicated regulations with such subjective and undefined standards as "fair balance," "significant information," "reliable studies" and "brief summary" were confusing and threatening. After all, a product could be seized for advertising violations and adverse publicity would accompany any notice of improper promotion. Two major advertisers suspended journal advertising awaiting clarification of the rules. The pocket-sized journals, *Medical Economics* and *Modern Medicine*, converted to a page size comparable to that of *JAMA* to accommodate the need for expanded space for brief summary. PMA went to court to overturn such requirement as that the generic name appear every time with the brand name in promotional text.

For all the alarm sounded when the new regulations were first announced, and criticism in the trade press and at hearings held to examine the provisions the FDA had devised to implement Kefauver-Harris, the industry and its advertising agencies eventually learned to live within this restrictive promotional environment. PMA won its case on generic name appearance but the other aspects of the new regulations went unchallenged. Pharmaceutical manufacturers soon saw the commercial logic of avoiding confrontation with the FDA over promotional rules when this agency also held the power of approval on new drugs worth millions in sales. Moreover, as the industry proceeded under Kefauver-Harris—preclearing with FDA introductory campaigns on new drugs, and observing how the rules would be interpreted through a series of actions that the FDA took against promotions judged to be in violation—advertisers and their agencies became adept in producing effective promotion within the 1963 guidelines.

Over the years, FDA has expanded its control over promotion, case by case, extending, for example, to such things as press releases and medical education. It was not until 1992, when the FDA attempted to govern continuing medical education with extensive regulations, that manufacturers' First Amendment rights to distribute truthful information, exempt from FDA clearance or scrutiny, became an issue and the FDA's power and role in information dissemination was challenged in the courts by the Washington Legal Foundation.

Since Kefauver-Harris, pharmaceutical advertising has been one of the most regulated fields of commercial promotion. Regardless of this inhibiting influence—requiring, for example, the display on all materials of a brief summary, which grew in most instances into a one- or two-page full disclosure—medical advertising and medical advertising agencies thrived in the 1960's. Fundamental to the expansion of medical advertising was the continued, phenomenal success of agency clients, the pharmaceutical manufacturers. The wonder drugs of the 1950's were followed by comparable advances in the 1960's. The period saw the first $100,000,000 brand, Valium (Roche) and as sales grew so did promotional budgets. Suffice to say, the regulatory burdens imposed did not succeed in diverting the investment or reducing the impact of advertising and promotion to prescribing audiences.

PAUL KLEMTNER (1905—1997)

Among the founders of early medical advertising agencies, Paul Klemtner stands out for his prowess as a business man in contrast to the more typical creative background of his peers. Klemtner's expertise was accounting and finance and it was in his capacity as a consultant on marketing operations that he first came into prominence. In the late 1930's, he recommended that companies redirect their sales forces from calls on dispensing physicians and pharmacists to MDs who were prescribers of patented, brand-name products and to reduce product lines and concentrate on the more profitable brands. This was sound advice for an industry that was changing from generic products to "specialty" drugs—the fruits of more advanced scientific research. It was logical that he would expand his consulting services to include advertising and promotion and he set up an agency in 1942.

He prided himself in delegating the creative side to others but he took a keen interest in new technology for medical communications. He championed audio-visual projects and pioneered cassettes and LP records for medical education. At his initiative, the agency conducted the first closed-circuit TV broadcast to physicians. He sold Lilly on televising the announcement of the findings of the Salk polio trials. Fifty-thousand physicians attended the event at 50 locations, in what is probably still a record for a TV project of this kind.

Klemtner, always a precise planner, had as his goal retiring at age 60, and he did so in 1965, selling shares of the agency to the managerial group. He moved to Florida for what proved an extended retirement, passing away at age 92 in 1997.

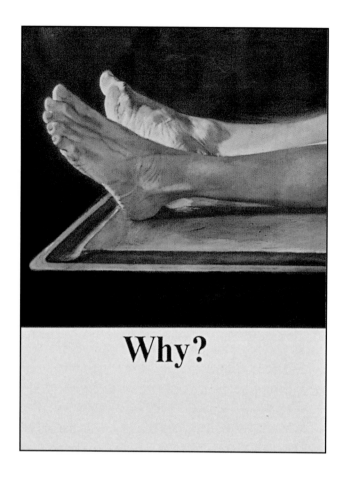

Why?

The *Client* (Warner-Chilcott) asked the *Agency* (Sudler & Hennessey) for an ad that would revive interest in Mandelamine, still an effective urinary antiseptic, even with the advent of antibiotics. The *Copywriter* (Mel Altshuler) and *Illustrator* (Arthur Lidov) created the most controversial ad in pharmaceutical history. (1953)

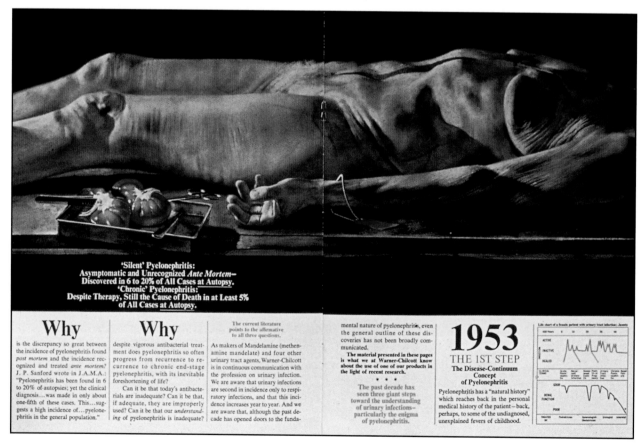

'Silent' Pyelonephritis:
Asymptomatic and Unrecognized *Ante Mortem*—
Discovered in 6 to 20% of All Cases at Autopsy.
'Chronic' Pyelonephritis:
Despite Therapy, Still the Cause of Death in at Least 5%
of All Cases at Autopsy.

Why

is the discrepancy so great between the incidence of pyelonephritis found *post mortem* and the incidence recognized and treated *ante mortem?* J. P. Sanford wrote in J.A.M.A.: "Pyelonephritis has been found in 6 to 20% of autopsies; yet the clinical diagnosis...was made in only about one-fifth of these cases. This...suggests a high incidence of...pyelonephritis in the general population."

Why

despite vigorous antibacterial treatment does pyelonephritis so often progress from recurrence to recurrence to chronic end-stage pyelonephritis, with its inevitable foreshortening of life?

Can it be that today's antibacterials are inadequate? Can it be that, if adequate, they are improperly used? Can it be that our *understanding* of pyelonephritis is inadequate?

The current literature points to the affirmative to all three questions.

As makers of Mandelamine (methenamine mandelate) and four other urinary tract agents, Warner-Chilcott is in continuous communication with the profession on urinary infection. We are aware that urinary infections are second in incidence only to respiratory infections, and that this incidence increases year to year. And we are aware that, although the past decade has opened doors to the fundamental nature of pyelonephritis, even the general outline of these discoveries has not been broadly communicated.

The material presented in these pages is what we at Warner-Chilcott know about the use of one of our products in the light of recent research.

* * *

The past decade has seen three giant steps toward the understanding of urinary infections—particularly the enigma of pyelonephritis.

1953
THE 1ST STEP
The Disease-Continuum
Concept
of Pyelonephritis

Pyelonephritis has a "natural history" which reaches back in the personal medical history of the patient—back, perhaps, to some of the undiagnosed, unexplained fevers of childhood.

when cough

MUST

be prevented!
Cough has a capacity for destruction ranging all the
way from respiratory complications to dehiscence
after abdominal surgery, from the stress fracture
of ribs in pregnancy and in asthma to the sudden
attack, sometimes fatal, of cough syncope. And in
ocular surgery and herniotomy, cough can even un-
do the operation itself. **Romilar**
non-narcotic cough specific...stops cough

"Heard melodies are sweet, but those unheard are sweeter"

NOLUDAR 300
DEEP, SATISFYING SLEEP WITH AN ALERT AWAKENING

How does a pomegranate taste?

It tastes like a pomegranate. No adjective could describe this
unique fruit to a person who's never tasted it; none, except
perhaps the word, "different."

The Librium Effect is difficult to describe—it, too, is "different." A patient treated with Librium feels different, even
after a few doses. He appears different to his family and to
his physician. Different, not only in the sense of a change
from the previous state of anxiety and tension. But also
freed from the sensations created by day-time sedatives
or tranquilizers. That the striking difference was first observed in a series of ingenious animal experiments is mainly
of theoretical interest. Of more practical importance, for
example, is that Librium lacks any depressant effect—a fact

which can assume overriding clinical importance. And this
is but one of the ways in which the difference can be observed.

Librium (like the pomegranate) deserves to be studied at first
hand. Why not select twelve patients who show emotional
or somatic signs of anxiety and tension, place six of them
on Librium—and see the difference in effect for yourself.

LIBRIUM
THE SUCCESSOR TO THE TRANQUILIZERS

1 *CLIENT:* Roche. *AGENCY:* McAdams.
AD: Jerry Philips. *COPY:* John Kallir (1960).
2 *CLIENT:* Roche. *AGENCY:* McAdams.
AD: Jerry Philips. *COPY:* John Kallir (1960).
3 *CLIENT:* Roche. *AGENCY:* McAdams.
AD: Jerry Philips. *ILLUSTR.:* Bill Charmatz. (1960).

1 *CLIENT:* Bristol. *AGENCY:* Sudler & Hennessey.
AD and *COPY:* Herb Lubalin (1960s).
2 *CLIENT:* Roche. *AGENCY:* McAdams.
AD: Jerry Philips. *PHOTOG.:* Gerald Hochman.
COPY: John Kallir (1960). **3** The most successful
campaign in the history of medical advertising
began in 1965 with fractional b/w pages in a
few medical journals. *Safer than aspirin, but
just as effective . . .* an obvious positioning in
retrospect, but it had never been tried before.
As Tylenol sales responded, budgets were
increased, but the product continued to be
promoted exclusively to physicians and
nurses from 1965 to 1975. By the time
consumer media were added to the mix, Tylenol
had become the leading non-Rx analgesic!
CLIENT: McNeil. *AGENCY:* Kallir Philips, Ross.
AD: Jerry Philips. *COPY:* Warren Ross. (1965).
4 *CLIENT:* Bristol. *AGENCY:* Sudler & Hennessey.
AD: Herb Lubalin. (1960s)

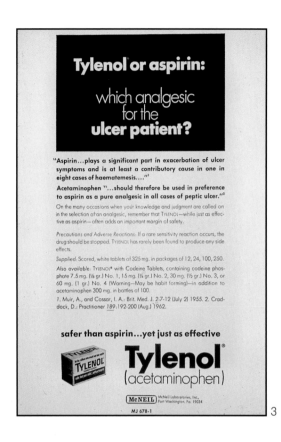

3

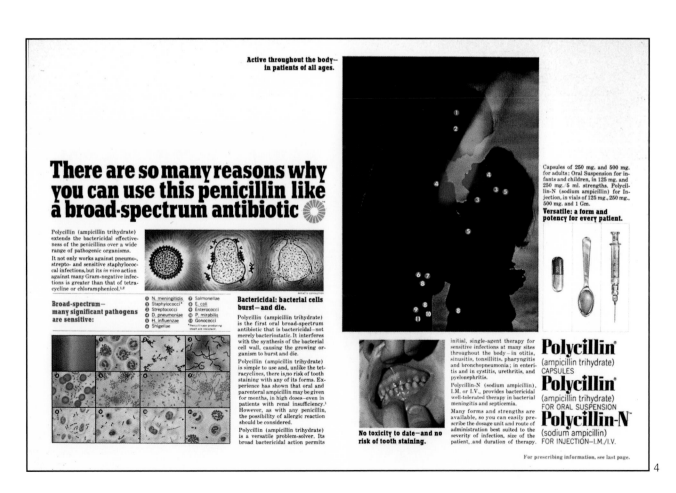

4

in an age
of discovery
step
beyond
the
thiazides

Space photographs courtesy of the
National Aeronautics and Space Administration.

1, 2 *CLIENT:* Hoechst.
AGENCY: L. W. Frohlich.
AD: Roger Core.
PHOTOG: NASA. (1966).
3 *CLIENT:* PFIZER.
AGENCY: Sudler & Hennessey.
AD: Herb Lubalin.
PHOTOG.: Art Kane. (1964).

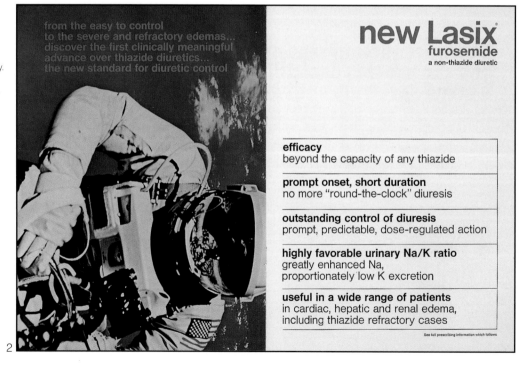

from the easy to control
to the severe and refractory edemas...
discover the first clinically meaningful
advance over thiazide diuretics...
the new standard for diuretic control

new Lasix
furosemide
a non-thiazide diuretic

efficacy
beyond the capacity of any thiazide

prompt onset, short duration
no more "round-the-clock" diuresis

outstanding control of diuresis
prompt, predictable, dose-regulated action

highly favorable urinary Na/K ratio
greatly enhanced Na,
proportionately low K excretion

useful in a wide range of patients
in cardiac, hepatic and renal edema,
including thiazide refractory cases

See full prescribing information which follows

MEDIA AND MARKETING RESEARCH

Marketing audits and research services on pharmaceuticals had developed in response to the promotional boom of the 1950's. During this period, Ray Gosselin, taking the idea he had investigated for his master's thesis in pharmacy school, began tracking Rx purchases at the retail level; Harry Knox launched a service that monitored promotional expenditures in journals, direct mail and detailing; and most importantly, Lea Associates in 1956 began comprehensive research among physicians on diagnosis and prescribing—the National Drug and Therapeutic Index (NDTI). The increase in pharmaceutical advertising and promotional budgets in the 1960's saw a movement of clients and agencies toward greater efficiency in allocation of funds using these and other data services.

Research techniques from consumer advertising were increasingly applied to the Rx field. In 1962 Mark Dresden with Sam Davis launched Media-Chek, a syndicated survey of medical journal readership linked to prescribing patterns and preferences.

to cover a multitude of skins

In many dermatoses, therapeutic baths are the most efficient (as well as the most pleasant) way of "getting at" the affected areas. This is particularly true when the condition is generalized or relatively inaccessible.

With Aveeno® bath products, your patient gets the antipruritic, anti-inflammatory benefits of time-tested colloidal oatmeal, while avoiding the bother once associated with colloid bath therapy.

in acute, wet dermatoses—
soothing baths with Aveeno Colloidal Oatmeal...cleanse and buffer the skin, allay itching and inflammation. Indicated in prickly heat, infantile eczema and diaper rash, intertrigo, poison ivy, sunburn, drug eruptions.

in dry, chronic dermatoses—
soothing baths with Aveeno Oilated...relieve irritation and restore skin moisture through a unique combination of colloidal oatmeal and 35% emollient oils. Indicated in senile pruritus, winter itch, bath itch, chronic atopic and contact dermatitis, as well as for symptomatic relief of pruritus in chicken pox and measles.

Aveeno Colloidal Oatmeal

Aveeno Oilated

Send for samples: Generous trial samples are available on request. Send for samples soon, both you and your patients will be pleased with the results.

Available: Aveeno Colloidal Oatmeal—1 lb. 2 oz. and 4 lb. boxes. One cup per bath is the average adult dosage.

Aveeno Oilated—10 oz. cans. Three to four tablespoonfuls per bath is the average adult dosage.

AVEENO DERMATOLOGICALS
Harrison, N. J.

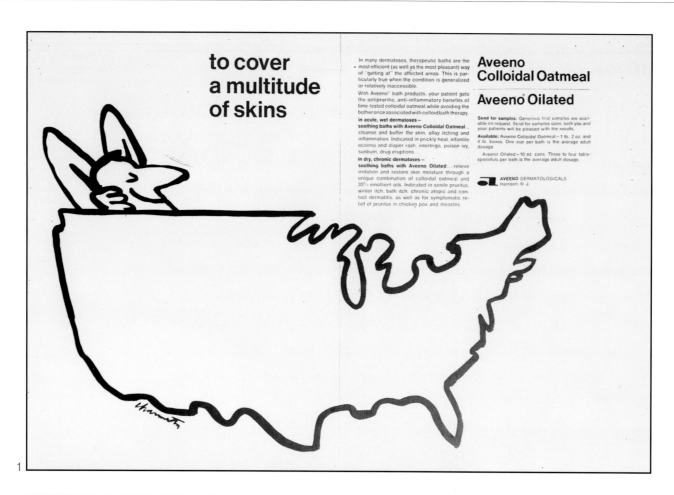

help keep her this way

specifically designed for the menopause...and the later years

Premarin
(CONJUGATED ESTROGENS - equine)

A growing trend

There is a growing trend toward treating the menopause as an estrogen deficiency state.[1-6] The idea is not new, of course, but is the logical development of a theory expressed nearly 25 years ago by Dr. Fuller Albright, a leading endocrinologist at Harvard Medical School.

Albright and associates noted "the constant tendency of osteoporosis to occur in women after the menopause" and the beneficial effect of estrogen therapy, and theorized that since the postmenopausal state was a common etiologic factor in osteoporosis, this condition was somehow related to ovarian insufficiency.[7]

During the quarter of a century since Albright's discovery, clinical experience has revealed that the distressing symptoms of the menopause and many metabolic disorders of the postmenopause are likewise related to failing ovarian function. It has also become widely recognized that early institution of adequate natural estrogen replacement therapy can provide prompt relief of physical and emotional distress, and protection against premature degenerative metabolic changes.

In the opinion of one contemporary authority,[4] estrogen replacement therapy has become accepted medical practice because "there is a growing realization that it is both morally and medically justifiable to make what has become almost half of a woman's life [the postmenopause] comfortable, healthy, and productive."

Avoid the consequences of estrogen deficiency

Menopausal flashes, flushes, sweats, and palpitations are familiar findings readily related to short term estrogen deficiency. Others include headache, insomnia, easy fatigability, and a psychologically negative attitude. But the consequences of prolonged estrogen deprivation are usually manifest in profound cosmetic and metabolic changes affecting the skin, the vaginal mucosa, bone, muscles and ligaments, causing the appearance of a "dowager's hump" and progressive loss of height due to osteoporosis, as well as loss of natural protection against coronary disease.

Today, menopausal distress can be promptly relieved and the consequences of long term ovarian insufficiency generally avoided, through the use of a continuing and cyclic estrogen replacement program to compensate for withdrawal of natural estrogen secretion.

(continued) ▶

Readership/exposure research became common practice across the range of media used in pharmaceutical promotion. Companies specializing in testing physician response to pharmaceutical ads and creative concepts (Palshaw, 1968) made their appearance and were employed by clients to validate product messages and to explore the underpinnings and behavioral dynamics of prescribers. Reliable data on company sales, spending on detailing, medical journal advertising and direct mail became available and more centralized in 1968 when Lea acquired the Gosselin and Knox service. L.W. Frohlich founded Intercontinental Marketing Services (IMS) and displaying his international outlook, began audits of European markets and also in 1968 purchased Davee, Kohnlein, and Keating (DKK)—a drug store and hospital audit of the U.S.—making IMS a global prescription data company. In 1972, IMS merged with Lea for a further consolidation of market information sources.

MATTHEW J. HENNESSEY

"Matt" Hennessey was "present at the creation" of modern medical advertising. In fact, he was one of the creators. In the 1950's he and his partner Arthur Sudler made Sudler & Hennessey—which had begun as an art studio— into the "hot" agency renowned for the excellence of its creative work.

Hennessey had a remarkable ability for recruiting and developing talent—writers, artists, designers, account and marketing people. As evidence of this ability, no fewer than eight major medical agencies were founded by executives who had come under his tutelage and numerous others went on to managerial positions in the industry. This steady departure of talent, however, in no way impeded the continuing growth of S&H, which for a span of 20 years from the 1970's to the 1990's was the largest medical agency in the U.S.

This outstanding success of S&H, which Hennessey managed on his own after Sudler's death in 1968, can be attributed to Hennessey's philosophy of assembling top-notch account teams and then pushing them beyond the limits of conventional advertising.

Beginning in the art department of Squibb in 1934 and retiring in 1984, Hennessey influenced a half-century of medical advertising. The "culture of excellence" he nurtured at S&H has left an indelible mark on the field.

1 *CLIENT:* Aveeno. *AGENCY:* Kallir, Philips, Ross. *ILLUSTR.:* Bill Charmatz. *COPY:* Jay Lilker. (1963).
2 *CLIENT:* Ayerst. *AGENCY:* Klemtner. *AD:* Bob Buechert. *COPY:* Harry Sweeney.

Decisions on message and media, once the province of "judgment," now had to deal with "the numbers" and the computer. This change was dramatized all the more in 1972 with the creation of PERQ by David Gideon, which provided on-line computer systems to assist with media selection, competitive ad tracking, and schedule management. This trend continued with the formation of Health Industries Research by David Labson shortly thereafter, offering both media readership, ad exposure research and reach-frequency analysis. The *art* of medical advertising had relinquished some of its prerogatives to the *science* of medical adverting.

Consumer advertising agencies have always been players on "Medicine Avenue," obtaining Rx business through corporate connection and then melding the accounts into their normal departmental organization. When billings were large enough, separate units were set up as was the case with the Wallace Laboratories account at Ted Bates. Because Wallace operated without sales representatives making calls on physicians, spending on journal advertising and direct mail was heavy, particularly the latter. It was not unusual for a physician to receive a mailing a day on Miltown or Milpath. The medical group at Bates developed Rx advertising expertise and used it in the 1960's to win assignments in competition with the specialized ethical drug agencies.

The growing lucrative pharmaceutical area attracted interest from others on Madison Avenue. J. Walter Thompson (JWT) brought James Barnum—a consumer marketer who became a physician after a successful career in product development—into the field in 1967 to head up a unit named Deltakos. The keystone account was Eli Lilly. Benton & Bowles (B&B) and Leo Burnett also tested the waters of Rx advertising in the 1950's–1960's but without success. These forays into pharmaceutical advertising by large consumer agencies were harbingers of the future.

The 70's

New Names on "Medicine Avenue"

Agency proliferation accelerated in the 1970's with the unexpected breakup of the Frohlich agency and departures from the older agencies greatly expanding the roster of "Medicine Avenue."

AGENCY PROLIFERATION

In 1971, the Rx advertising scene was disrupted by the untimely death of L.W. Frohlich and the breakup of his agency, which had been one of the largest in the U.S. and, when the overseas offices were included, the biggest in the world. The American agency closed its doors in 1972 but the branches in Europe and Japan continued. Two new agencies emerged from the Frohlich partition: Medicus Communications formed by V. Edward Dent, William G. Castagnoli and Lawrence Lesser as a joint venture with B&B, and Lavey/Wolff/Swift named for its founders Kenneth Lavey, Bruce Wolff and John Swift. Both agencies would become significant players in medical advertising.

Although Medicus and L/W/S came about from the demise of one of the founder agencies, proliferation of medical agencies did not depend on the failure of organizations that had established the field in the 1950's. The robust growth of pharmaceutical advertising created opportunities for new agencies and the older shops became the training ground for talented individuals who "went out on their own." Sudler & Hennessey proved to be a particularly fertile field in nurturing "Medicine Avenue" entrepreneurs. It was the source of Dorland, Sweeney, Jones (Harry Sweeney and Dick Jones) 1971, Dugan/Farley (John Farley, Clay Warrington and Martin Ross) 1974, Ferguson Communications (Thomas Ferguson) 1974, Dorritie, Lyons, Nickel (John Dorritie, Michael Lyons, and Albert Nickel) 1979, and Lally McFarland Pantello (John Lally, Jim McFarland and Ron Pantello) 1980.

Rolf W. Rosenthal left McAdams in 1972 to found his agency (RWR) and, to add to the growing number of medical agencies, James Barnum, after a dispute with JWT management, set up Barnum Communications in 1977. Barnum's legal clash with JWT closed the Deltakos office in San Francisco. Principals from that agency—Robert Buechert, Reginald Bowes, Lester Barnett, Jerry Kennedy, Thomas Spooner and John Roche—came together to found Vicom (1977) in San Francisco becoming, with Baxter, Gurian & Mazzei (1968) in Southern California, West Coast outposts of pharmaceutical advertising. Some of the Vicom founders had previously worked for the branch office of Klemtner that had been opened in 1965 to serve such Bay Area clients as Syntex and Barnes Hind.

Other significant foundings in this period were Gross, Townsend, Frank, Hoffman (1978), Salthouse, Torre, Ferrante (1979), Bologna (1980), and Sutton

1 *CLIENT:* Stuart. *AGENCY:* Sudler & Hennessey.
AD: Steve Brothers. *ILLUSTR.:* Tomi Ungerer. (1971).
2 *CLIENT:* Ortho. *AGENCY:* Kallir, Philips, Ross.
AD: Al Zalon. *COPY:* Al Gerstein. (1974).

If gas is keeping her up

If gas pain and discomfort make her restive by day... and night...consider Mylicon. It's an effective, single-entity antiflatulent.

Mylicon safely disperses foamy mucus that entraps G.I. gas—thus freeing the gas for easier expulsion.* And, as the gas goes....so go the pain and discomfort.

*except in the case of major obstruction

Each Mylicon tablet or 0.6 ml. of drops contains 40 mg. of simethicone. Tablets should be chewed thoroughly for best results. Mylicon drops permit dosage flexibility. They may be given directly to the patient or added to oral fluids.

STUART PHARMACEUTICALS | Pasadena, Calif. 91109
Division of ATLAS CHEMICAL INDUSTRIES, INC.

Mylicon® (simethicone)

Fits into their world...

An effective low-dose oral contraceptive

Ortho-Novum 1/50 □ 21

Each tablet contains 1 mg norethindrone and 0.05 mg mestranol

A sensible way to start a woman on oral contraceptives is with an effective, low-dose combination like Ortho-Novum 1/50 □ 21.

This combination offers a low dose of estrogen, 50 mcg of mestranol,

and a low dose of progestin, 1 mg norethindrone, which can fulfill your contraceptive requirements and her contraceptive needs.

Ortho-Novum 1/50 □ 21 is usually a well-tolerated* combination;

thus, in clinical studies there is a low drug-related drop-out rate.

Add to this the simplicity of the dosage regimen—three weeks on and one week off—and the unique Dialpak! Tablet Dispenser, which

helps reduce the chance of error or missed doses, and you have an effective combination that fits very nicely into their life-style... and their world.

*See prescribing information on following page

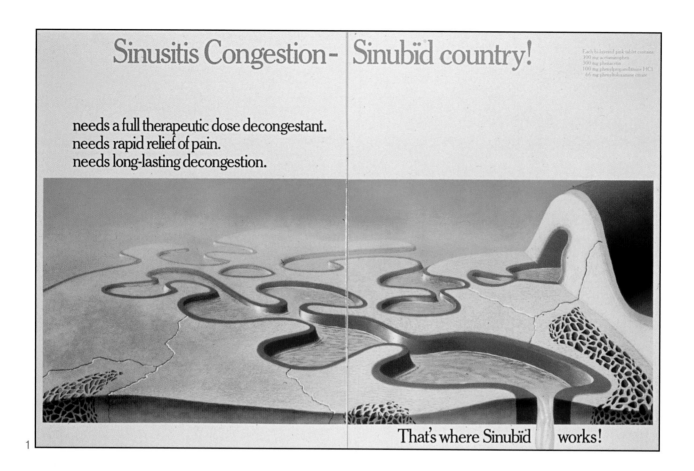

1

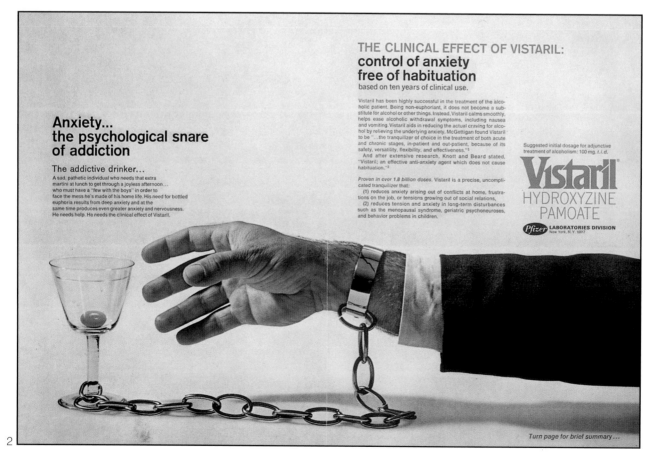

2

1 *CLIENT:* Warner-Chilcott. *AGENCY:* Sudler & Hennessey.
AD: Frank Wagner. *ILLUSTR.:* Don Ivan Punchatz. (1974).
2 *CLIENT:* Pfizer. *AGENCY:* Sudler & Hennessey.
AD: Arthur Ludwig 3 *CLIENT:* Upjohn. *AGENCY:* Kallir,
Philips, Ross. *AD:* Jerry Philips. *ILLUSTR.:* Lou Bori. (1974).
4 *CLIENT:* Pharmacia. *AGENCY:* Shaller-Rubin.
AD: Patrick O'Connor. *COPY:* Frank Hughes. (1973).

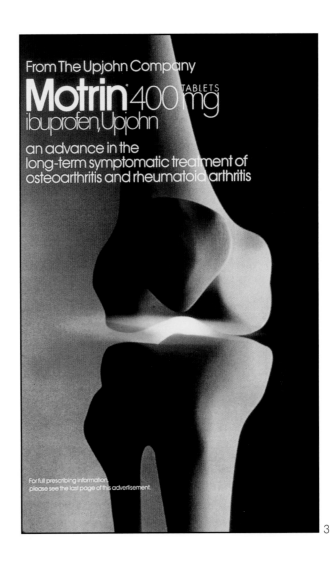

3

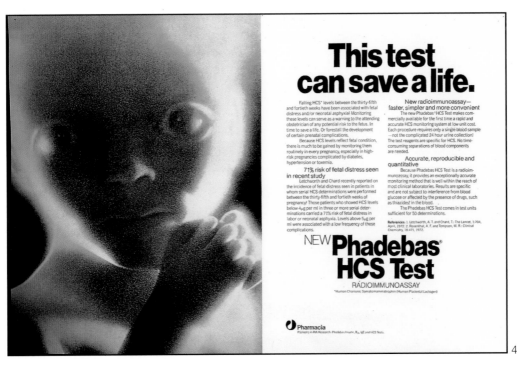

4

(1982). Competition in medical advertising was intensifying as new agencies developed from the pool of writers, art directors, and account personnel created at the older agencies by the expanding funds pharmaceutical manufacturers invested in advertising and promotion. For example, medical journal advertising had totaled $86 million in 1966 and had gone to $102 million by 1971 and to $132 million by 1976. Similar increases were seen in other areas of pharmaceutical promotion as companies added sales representatives, conducted pre-launch information programs to assist the introduction of new products, and utilized a wide range of other media to compete for physicians' attention.

In 1972, Frank Corbett sold his agency to the consumer giant Batton, Barton, Durstin & Osborne (BBD&O)—the same year B&B invested in Medicus. Along with JWT's Deltakos, these were the principal consumer agencies in the field in the 1970's (Ted Bates had discontinued its medical section). The Corbett sale marked the beginning of a trend that would see virtually all major medical agencies purchased by large consumer agencies as these organizations diversified broadly into a range of communication services.

1 *CLIENT:* Pfizer Roerig.
AGENCY: Sudler & Hennessey.
AD: Mike Lyons.
PHOTOG: John Conboy,
COPY: Jane Sarnoff
2 *CLIENT:* Key.
AGENCY: Bologna Intl.
AD: Mark McDowell.
COPY: Frank Hughes. (1980).
3 *CLIENT:* Key.
AGENCY: Bologna Intl.
AD: Mark McDowell.
COPY: Frank Hughes. (1980).

If he's making the
rounds of San Francisco...

Antivert
(meclizine HCl)
for vertigo*

Antivert* (meclizine HCl) has been found useful in the management of vertigo associated with diseases affecting the vestibular system. It is available as Antivert (12.5 mg. meclizine HCl) and Antivert/25 (25 mg. meclizine HCl) scored tablets for convenience and flexibility of dosage. Antivert/25 (25 mg. meclizine HCl) Chewable Tablets are available for the management of nausea, vomiting, and dizziness associated with motion sickness.

*INDICATIONS. Based on a review of this drug by the National Academy of Sciences-National Research Council and/or other information, FDA has classified the indications as follows:
Effective: Management of nausea and vomiting and dizziness associated with motion sickness.
Possibly Effective: Management of vertigo associated with diseases affecting the vestibular system.
Final classification of the less than effective indications requires further investigation.

CONTRAINDICATIONS. Administration of Antivert during pregnancy or to women who may become pregnant is contraindicated in view of the teratogenic effect of the drug in rats.
The administration of meclizine to pregnant rats during the 12th-15th day of gestation has produced cleft palate in the offspring. Limited studies using doses of over 100 mg./kg./day in rabbits and 10 mg./kg./day in pigs and monkeys did not show cleft palate. Congeners of meclizine have caused cleft palate in species other than the rat.
Meclizine HCl is contraindicated in individuals who have shown a previous hypersensitivity to it.

WARNINGS. Since drowsiness may, on occasion, occur with use of this drug, patients should be warned of this possibility and cautioned against driving a car or operating dangerous machinery.
Usage in Children: Clinical studies establishing safety and effectiveness in children have not been done; therefore, usage is not recommended in the pediatric age group.
Usage in Pregnancy: See "Contraindications."

ADVERSE REACTIONS. Drowsiness, dry mouth and, on rare occasions, blurred vision have been reported.

A division of Pfizer Pharmaceuticals
New York, New York 10017

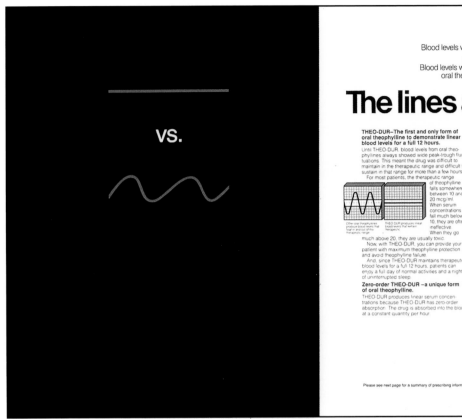

VS.

Blood levels with THEO-DUR*
anhydrous theophylline
vs.
Blood levels with other forms of
oral theophylline:

The lines are drawn.

THEO-DUR—The first and only form of oral theophylline to demonstrate linear blood levels for a full 12 hours.

Until THEO-DUR, blood levels from oral theophyllines always showed wide peak-trough fluctuations. This meant the drug was difficult to maintain in the therapeutic range and difficult to sustain in that range for more than a few hours.

For most patients, the therapeutic range of theophylline falls somewhere between 10 and 20 mcg/ml. When serum concentrations fall much below 10, they are often ineffective. When they go much above 20, they are usually toxic.

Now, with THEO-DUR, you can provide your patient with maximum theophylline protection and avoid theophylline failure.

And, since THEO-DUR maintains therapeutic blood levels for a full 12 hours, patients can enjoy a full day of normal activities and a night of uninterrupted sleep.

Zero-order THEO-DUR—a unique form of oral theophylline.

THEO-DUR produces linear serum concentrations because THEO-DUR has zero-order absorption. The drug is absorbed into the blood at a constant quantity per hour.

Other oral forms of theophylline have first-order absorption, in which the largest amount is absorbed in the first hour and proportionately smaller amounts thereafter.

When absorption varies, as it does with first-order drugs, protection can also vary. That's why first-order theophyllines can be toxic within the first few hours and subtherapeutic later on.

THEO-DUR—the practical benefits.

Your patient benefits from the maximum control provided by THEO-DUR in several important ways: exercise tolerance is increased, emergency hospital visits are less likely and concomitant therapy is usually unnecessary.

Dosage titration is easy to achieve* THEO-DUR is the only sustained-action tablet in 200 mg as well as 100 and 300 mg strengths and all tablets are scored for greater dosage flexibility.

THEO-DUR also enhances patient compliance—with an every 12 hour dosage schedule that's easier to remember.

*After three days, on a steady dose, serum concentrations should be monitored and appropriate dosage adjustments made, if necessary.

THEO-DUR®
anhydrous theophylline
Sustained Action Tablets

Today's most widely-prescribed bronchodilator.

KEY PHARMACEUTICALS, INC.

Please see next page for a summary of prescribing information.

We straightened out the problem of theophylline blood levels.

THEO-DUR* (anhydrous theophylline)—The first and only form of oral theophylline to demonstrate linear blood levels for a full 12 hours.

The problem with theophylline blood levels is that they are difficult to maintain in the therapeutic range and difficult to sustain for more than a few hours.

For most patients, the therapeutic range of theophylline is somewhere between 10 and 20 mcg/ml. If serum concentrations fall much below 10, theophylline is often ineffective. If they go much above 20, they are usually toxic.

THEO-DUR is the only form of oral theophylline to offer linear serum concentrations. It minimizes the peak-trough fluctuations common to many other oral theophyllines. Once titrated, linear serum concentrations assure that THEO-DUR will remain therapeutic.

And, since THEO-DUR maintains therapeutic blood levels for 12 hours, patients can enjoy a full day of normal activities and a night of uninterrupted sleep.

Zero-order THEO-DUR—a unique form of oral theophylline.

THEO-DUR produces linear serum concentrations because THEO-DUR has zero-order absorption. The drug is absorbed into the blood at a constant quantity per hour.

Other oral forms of theophylline have first-order absorption, in which the largest amount is absorbed in the first hour and proportionately smaller amounts thereafter.

When absorption varies, as it does with first-order drugs, protection can also vary. That's why first-order theophyllines can be toxic within the first few hours and subtherapeutic later on.

THEO-DUR—the practical benefits.

Your patient benefits from the maximum control provided by THEO-DUR in several important ways: exercise tolerance is increased, emergency hospital visits are less likely and concomitant therapy is usually unnecessary.

Dosage titration is easy to achieve* THEO-DUR is the only sustained-action tablet in 200 mg as well as 100 and 300 mg strengths, and all tablets are scored for greater dosage flexibility.

THEO-DUR also enhances patient compliance—with an every 12 hour dosage schedule that's easier to remember.

*After three days, on a steady dose, serum concentrations should be monitored and appropriate dosage adjustments made, if necessary.

$$\frac{dc}{dt} = K$$

THEO-DUR®
anhydrous theophylline
Sustained Action Tablets

Today's most widely-prescribed bronchodilator.

KEY PHARMACEUTICALS, INC.

Please see next page for a summary of prescribing information.

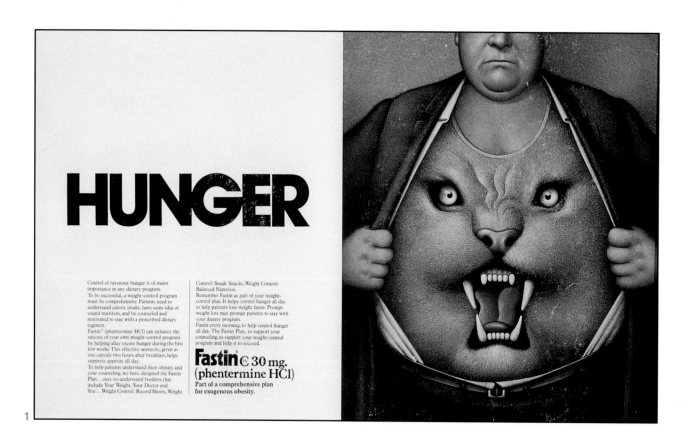

1 *CLIENT:* Beecham. *AGENCY:*
Corbett. *AD:* Dave Meade.
COPY: Don Courtney.
CS: Peter Zanet
2 *CLIENT:* Pfizer. *AGENCY:* Sudler
& Hennessey. *AD:* Mike Lyons.
COPY: John Lally. (1977).

64

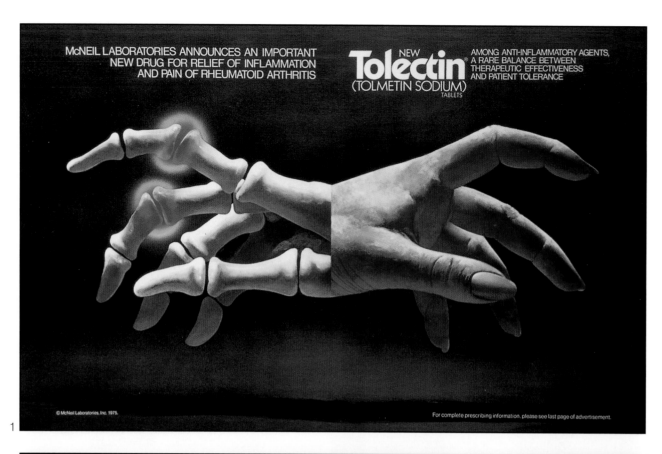

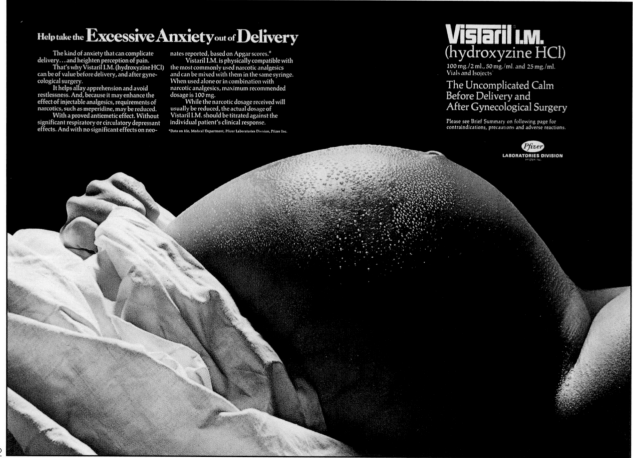

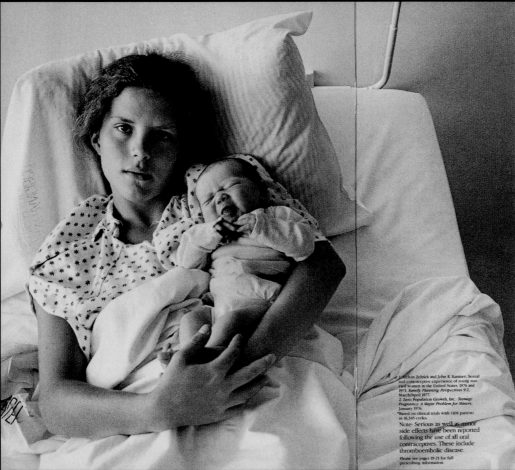

Sweet sixteen.

Not very long ago, "sweet sixteen" marked a meaningful milestone in the life of a young woman, a pinnacle in the passage from puberty to womanhood. Times have changed.

Today's society-in-flux is more complex, less clearly defined by traditional standards of conduct. As a result, today's sixteen-year-old may be anguished, without a sense of hope, instead of joyously celebrant and optimistic.

Consider the following. Today, it is estimated that 25% of young women have had intercourse by age sixteen.[1] And, today, teens are responsible for half of all out of wedlock births. Of these, some two-thirds are unplanned, unwanted.[2]

One thing is painfully clear. Teenage ignorance regarding sexuality is as prevalent as teenage sexual activity. Never before was there a more acute need for substantive instruction coupled with compassionate, reassuring counseling. As disturbing as it may be, many teens are also in need of basic contraceptive guidance. In each of these areas, the physician can play an enormously important role.

For many sexually active teenagers, the selection of a sub-50 mcg oral contraceptive, like Brevicon, can be a sound choice. Brevicon offers a rate of efficacy comparable to higher dose formulations and a well-accepted rate of menstrual irregularities. (Cycle incidence of breakthrough bleeding and amenorrhea is 5.1% and 1.0% respectively. Dropout rate due to menstrual irregularities is only 3.4% during the critical first three cycles.)*

Brevicon coupled with counseling, compassion and reassurance. Not a panacea, but one good way to help our teenagers avoid unwanted, unplanned births.

Make plans now to attend
Adolescent Sexuality:
Clinical Challenge of the Transitional Years
a nationwide symposium • live, closed-circuit telecast • to 10 major cities
March 26, 1980

Details available through your Syntex representative

Tablets
Brevicon®
(norethindrone 0.5 mg
with ethinyl
estradiol 0.035 mg)

**A sign of
the times.**

SYNTEX (F.P.), INC.
HUMACAO, P.R. 00661
© 1979 Syntex (F.P.), Inc.

1. Melvin Zelnick and John F. Kantner: Sexual and contraceptive experience of young married women in the United States, 1976 and 1971. *Family Planning Perspectives* 9:2, March/April 1977.
2. Zero Population Growth, Inc.: *Teenage Pregnancy: A Major Problem for Minors*, January 1976.
*Based on clinical trials with 1368 patients in 16,345 cycles.
Note: Serious as well as minor side effects have been reported following the use of all oral contraceptives. These include thromboembolic disease.
Please see pages 19-21 for full prescribing information.

3

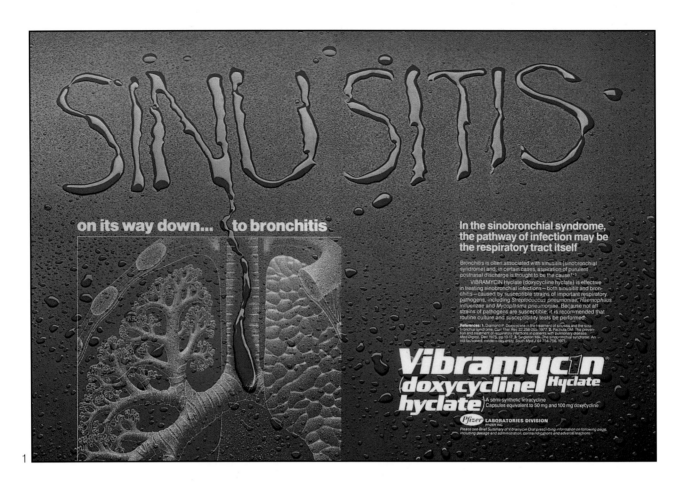

1 CLIENT: Pfizer. AGENCY: Klemtner .
AD: Clyde Davis. COPY: Karen Blunt
2 CLIENT: Dome. AGENCY: Lavey/Wolff/Swift.
AD: Mark McDowell. COPY:Bob Levine (1976).

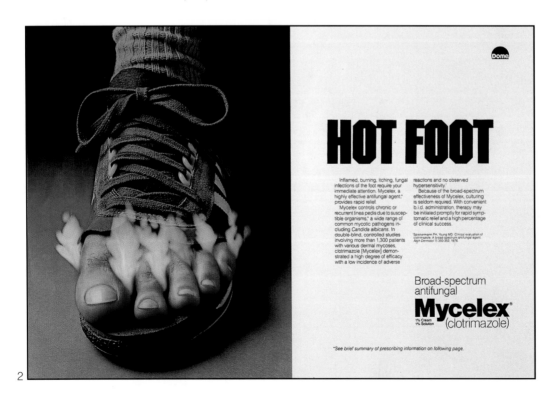

The 80's

Acquisitions, International Expansion, and DTC

The purchase of medical agencies by consumer agencies continued. American agencies furthered their overseas involvement. Direct-to-consumer advertising arrived to greatly expand the promotional mix.

ACQUISITIONS BY CONSUMER AGENCIES

Over the years, the number of independent medical agencies has been reduced. The "founder" agencies have been acquired: Sudler & Hennessey by Young & Rubicam in 1972, Klemtner by Compton in 1979, and McAdams by the Lowe Group, a unit of Interpublic, in 1996. Further, the offspring of these older agencies have also become parts of consumer agencies.

Other consumer agency acquisitions:

Robert E. Wilson—BBD&O, 1972

Lavey/Wolff/Swift—BBD&O, 1977

Kallir Philips Ross—Doyle Dane Bernbach, 1983

Vicom—Foote Cone & Belding, 1984

Rolf Werner Rosenthal—Ogilvy & Mather, 1984

Baxter Gurian Mazzei—Omnicom, 1986

Gross Townsend Frank & Hoffman—Grey, 1986

Sieber McIntyre—Interpublic, 1986

Robert A. Becker—EURO RSCG, 1987

Botto Roessner Horne & Messinger—Ketchum, 1988

Lally McFarland & Pantello—EURO RSCG, 1989

Sutton—Medicus, 1990

Ferguson—WPP Group, 1990

Harrison Star Wiener & Beitler—Omnicom, 1992

Dorritie Lyons Nickel—Omnicom, 1994

Dugan/Farley—Bozell, 1995

Lewis Gace—Bozell, 1995

Torre Lazur—Interpublic, 1996

Cline Davis & Mann—Omnicom, 1997

Intergrated—Interpublic, 1997

Pace—Interpublic, 1998

Toltzis—Jordan McGrath Case Partners, 1998

Grob—Interpublic, 1998

Sizable independent agencies as of 1998 with longevity in the field:

Vox (Ted Thomas 1953), Adair Green (1966), Hal Lewis (1967), Impact Communications (1969), Dorland Sweeney Jones (1971), Carrafiello-Diehl (1973), Gerbig Snell / Weisheimer (1977), Lanmark (1977), Lehman Millet (1978), Forsythe Marcelli Johnson (1980), K. I. Lipton (1980), Paul A. DeJesse (1980), Sturm Rosenberg King (1980), Abelson-Taylor (1981), Goble (1982), Topin (1982), Hamilton Communications (1982), Strategic Medical (1982), BBK (1983), BHS Group (1983), Lena Chow (1984), Sandler Communications (1984), Edward Newland (1985), AD-TECH (1985), Donahoe & Purohit (1985), Rockett Burkhead Lewis & Winslow (1985), KSP (1987), Barton & Pittinos (1988), Kingswood (1988), Nelson Communications (1988), Bryan Brown Maynard (1989), Falk (1989), Leverte (1989).

In 1997, GHBM Healthworld which had been founded by Steve Girgenti, Frank Hughes, William Butler, and Mark McDowell in 1986 became the first independent agency to go public with a stock offering.

Independents founded since 1990 are:

Creative Medical (1990), Communico (1990), Esprit (1990), Ribotsky (1990), Bruce Leeb (1991), Lawrence & Mayo (1991), Sandler & Recht (1991), Dudnyk (1992), BioGenesis (1993), Pacific Communications (1993), Harrison Wilson (1994), Sperling Sampson West (1994), Catalyst Communications (1996), Camp + Tate (1998).

CLIENT: Procter & Gamble.
AGENCY: Lally, McFarland & Pantello. *COPY:* Bernard Ward.
AD: Jim McFarland.

INTERNATIONAL GROWTH

Besides an increased corporate connection to consumer advertising conglomerates, another feature that characterizes American medical agencies in the 1980's and 1990's is their overseas expansion. L.W. Frohlich was a pioneer in this regard, setting up wholly owned subsidiaries in London, Frankfurt, Paris, Milan and Tokyo under the name L.W. Frohlich/Intercon. After Frohlich's death, the agency's offices in Europe and Asia dropped the Frohlich name and were known corporately as Intercon. Sudler & Hennessey also invested in the international field through a specialized unit, Arranz & Sudler, which in 1970 expanded its operations in Europe.

In 1980, the Medicus unit of B&B acquired the Intercon network and for a few years became, on the strength of these branches, the world's largest medical advertising agency. Soon others were buying or setting up agencies in Canada, Mexico, Europe, Asia and Australia or entering into joint ventures and cooperative arrangements with agencies in these regions. More and more American agencies were producing creative work for use or adaptation in marketing areas beyond the United States. As such, U.S. agencies exercised a strong influence on the style and technique of medical advertising outside this country, although this was not a one-way street since strong creative work from overseas was also gaining visibility here. Because clients are moving toward establishing pharmaceutical brands globally, it can be anticipated that the globalization of medical advertising will continue with U.S. agencies playing a leading role.

Another aspect of the American market with which American agencies have become involved and which has potential for export is expertise in selling to managed care organizations (MCOs). The early 1990's saw government and industry becoming advocates for MCO systems as a means of stemming the disturbing rise in the cost of healthcare. Pharmaceutical clients reacted by restructuring and decentralizing sales management, involving themselves with pharmaceutical benefit management companies (PBMs), initiating outcome and cost benefit studies, and a reordering of promotional priorities toward formulary acceptance. Agencies, likewise, staffed and reorganized for sales programs to MCOs. Sizable portions of the American market are governed by

MCO considerations, and as such, agencies have continued developing understanding and skills in how to sell Rx drugs to this class of customer. As the world adopts the managed care model this knowledge and experience is likely to be in demand.

DIRECT-TO-CONSUMER ADVERTISING

Coincidentally with the movement toward a smaller audience of decision makers on prescription drugs—formulary managers of MCOs—an entirely contrary development has greatly expanded communications on Rx products. This trend is advertising to the public—direct-to-consumer (DTC) advertising—which has changed the industry's outlook from exclusive concentration on professional audiences to inclusion of mass audiences of millions of consumers.

Experiments in DTC began in the early 1980's when the English company Boots Pharmaceuticals, which had licensed Motrin in this country to Upjohn, decided to compete against this highly successful anti-arthritic with its own brand of the product, Rufen. Its approach was a price comparison. The TV and print ads that ran in a test market in 1983 provoked a storm of criticism, comment, and prompt action by the FDA. Brand name advertising of prescription drugs to the public was not prohibited by the government regulation of the industry. It had never been addressed since the conventions of prescription drug advertising had, for more than 60 years, viewed such practices as unethical for the "ethical drug" industry. Merck had run pneumonia vaccine advertising in *Readers Digest* and other publications in 1981 but this was seen as a special, public health situation.

The first DTC ad appeared in Readers Digest in 1981. *CLIENT:* Merck. *AGENCY:* Kallir, Philips, Ross. *AD:* John Geryak. *COPY:* Dick Grossman.

FDA challenged the Rufen ads, forcing revisions to include the brief summary and fair balance. After brief exposure in the test market, Boots dropped the campaign, but the wall against consumer advertising had been breached. The action of Boots had called attention to the option of consumer advertising in Rx promotion. The precedent was not unobserved in marketing departments of other pharmaceutical companies. Shortly afterward, the FDA Commissioner, Arthur Hull Hayes, a member of the Reagan administration, which favored less government regulation of business, observed in a speech to an advertising audience that DTC was a legal avenue for pharmaceutical promotion. Again, a flood of objections surfaced from organized medicine, academe, Congress and the industry itself. In the face of this reaction, Hayes announced a two-year moratorium on DTC using brand names while FDA studied the situation.

Non-branded advertising, however, continued. A notable example was the print and TV campaign created by McAdams on behalf of Pfizer. Essentially public health messages about heart disease, diabetes and arthritis, the campaign encouraged potential patients to consult their physicians. Without mentioning brand names, the ads explained that drugs for those conditions were available from Pfizer. Their doctor might then decide to prescribe an appropriate Pfizer product. Merrell Dow through Medicus also took this "help-seeking" approach in marketing Nicorette, a smoking cessation chewing gum (1983), and Seldane, a non-sedating antihistamine (1984). The Pfizer and Merrell Dow products were successful and their success was attributed, in part, to DTC. As evidence of the experimentation in the field, GHBM in 1987 conducted a campaign for Minitran (3M), a nitroglycerin patch, which was the first DTC program with no parallel advertising to physicians.

In 1988, Upjohn, which had actively opposed Rufen's use of DTC, mounted an extensive DTC campaign for its male pattern baldness product, Rogaine. Another big boost for DTC was the introduction of the smoking cessation patches Habitrol (CIBA) and Nicoderm (Marion Merrell Dow) and ProStep (Lederle) in 1991.

Since then, DTC has mushroomed until expenditures by pharmaceutical companies in consumer media exceed those in medical journals. Spending in television, radio, print, outdoor, and the Internet for DTC will exceed the billion

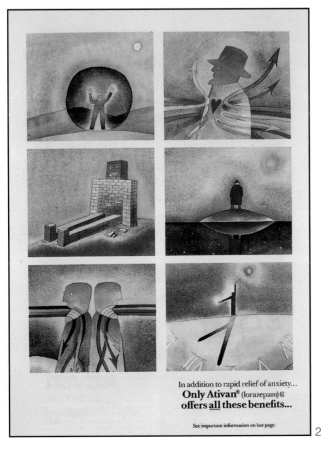

dollar level, it is estimated, in 1999. FDA's new regulation on DTC issued in 1997, which relaxed the brief summary requirement for TV, will likely encourage increased spending on DTC. Sizable percentages of DTC funds are gravitating to consumer agencies and their direct-marketing units. The growing market for DTC advertising is an impetus for consumer agencies to acquire medical agencies in order to gain access and expertise in pharmaceutical marketing and advertising. Likewise, medical agency ownership has seen the need for consumer agency association in order to compete for DTC business.

Consumer advertising has become a basic element in pharmaceutical promotion in the second half of this decade. All major Rx companies have conducted or are now conducting DTC campaigns. So it is that the pharmaceutical industry and its specialized advertising agencies, which once defined themselves by a marketing style that shunned advertising to the public, have come full circle, and ended in the surprising location of embracing the promotion of branded products to consumers. This does not mean that medical advertising will abandon its professional tone and scientific approach. It does indicate, however, that medical agencies will continue to expand their scope, going beyond healthcare professionals to lay audiences. If anything, the American medical agency in the late 1990's occupies a pivotal position in pharmaceutical marketing which, with the advent of more complex biotech products, requires even more of what Dr. Fishbein was looking for in a medical agency in 1926: "… advertising writers [consulting] vast amounts of controversial medical literature … sales of commodities on the basis of scientific evidence … logic that is logical … that will yield the best results for the public good."

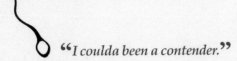

"*I coulda been a contender.*"

DEMULEN®1/35
(ethynodiol diacetate 1 mg, ethinyl estradiol 35 mcg)

Where protection begins

The physician should become familiar with the prescribing information (labeling) for this product, which discusses reported risks, such as thromboembolic disorders (including strokes and heart attacks), risk of estrogen dose, and hepatic lesions, as well as the need to monitor patients for early symptoms of any diseases or medical conditions, so use can be discontinued when appropriate.

Please see adjoining page for a brief summary of prescribing information.

The OC innovator   **SEARLE**

DUAL
ACTION
Triavil®
containing perphenazine and amitriptyline HCl

helps treat both
depression and moderate anxiety

an antidepressant alone may not be enough

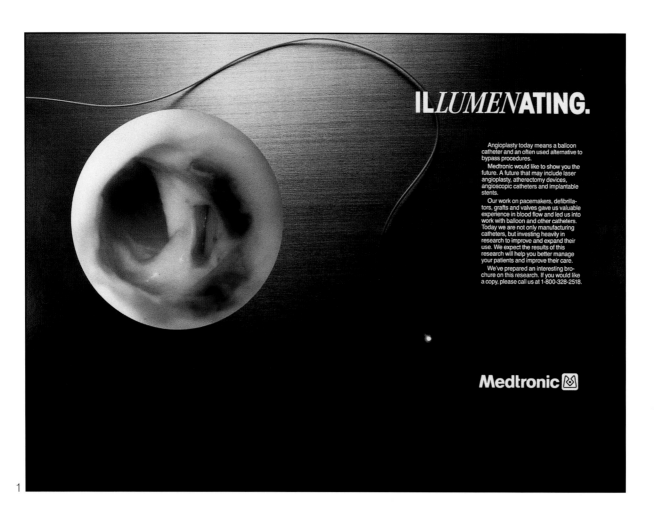

IL*LUMEN*ATING.

Angioplasty today means a balloon catheter and an often used alternative to bypass procedures.

Medtronic would like to show you the future. A future that may include laser angioplasty, atherectomy devices, angioscopic catheters and implantable stents.

Our work on pacemakers, defibrillators, grafts and valves gave us valuable experience in blood flow and led us into work with balloon and other catheters. Today we are not only manufacturing catheters, but investing heavily in research to improve and expand their use. We expect the results of this research will help you better manage your patients and improve their care.

We've prepared an interesting brochure on this research. If you would like a copy, please call us at 1-800-328-2518.

Medtronic

1

NOTHING IS IMPASSABLE.

The goal of every angioplasty procedure is to reach, cross and dilate the symptomatic lesion.

Today the greatest limitation the physician faces in achieving that goal is the available technology. Consequently, areas of the coronary vasculature are difficult, but not impossible, to reach and cross.

Medtronic has been working diligently to improve angioplasty technologies and increase lesion access by providing greater tip flexibility, greater torque control and more sensitive handling, a slimmer balloon profile, a surface that slides more easily and a

catheter tip and shaft that are highly visible under fluoroscopy.

Two of these advanced balloon catheters, Omniflex™ and Thruflex™, are now available. If you would like more information on these products and Medtronic's ongoing angioplasty research, please call us at 1-800-328-2518.

Copyright © 1988 by Medtronic, Inc.

Medtronic

2

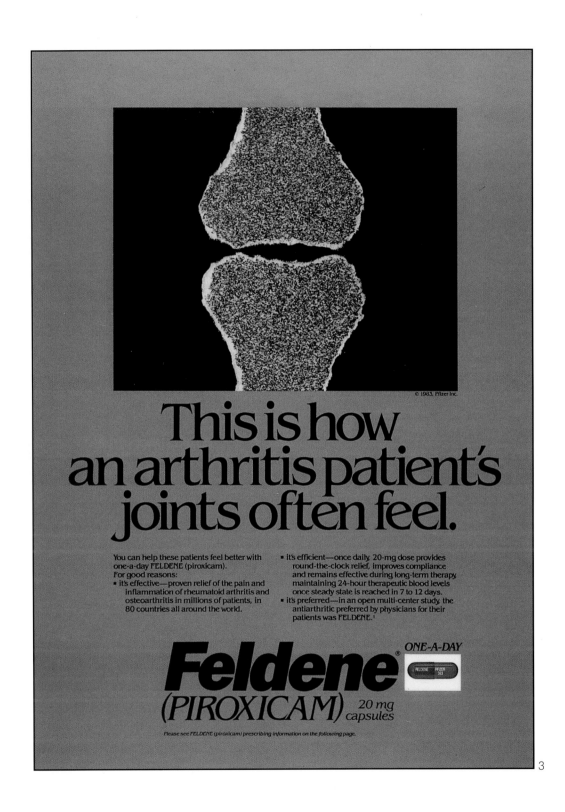

1, 2 *CLIENT:* Medtronic *AGENCY:*Bologna Intl.
AD: Mark McDowell. *COPY:* Frank Hughes.
3 *CLIENT:* Pfizer. *AGENCY:* Dorritie & Lyons.
AD: Mike Lyons *COPY:* Bill Brown (1983).

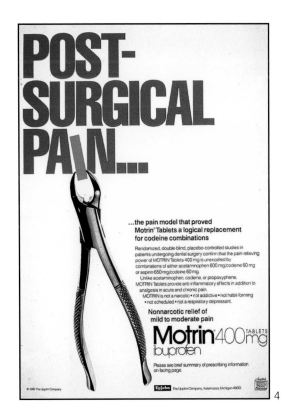

1 *CLIENT:* Roche. *AGENCY:* McAdams.
COPY: John Avery. *AD:* Tom Haynes
2 *CLIENT:* Procter & Gamble.
AGENCY: Lally, McFarland & Pantello.
*COPY:*John Lally. *AD:* Jim McFarland.
3 *CLIENT:* Smith Kline Beecham.
AGENCY: Salthouse Torre Norton. (1991).
4 *CLIENT:* Upjohn. *AGENCY:* Kallir,
Philips, Ross. *AD:* Jerry Philips.
COPY: Bernie Steinman. (1985).

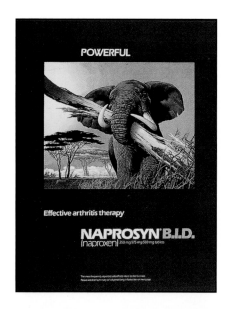

POWERFUL

Effective arthritis therapy

NAPROSYN B.I.D.
(naproxen) 250 mg/375 mg/500 mg tablets

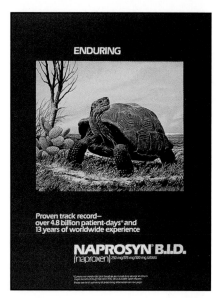

ENDURING

Proven track record—
over 4.8 billion patient-days* and
13 years of worldwide experience

NAPROSYN B.I.D.
(naproxen) 250 mg/375 mg/500 mg tablets

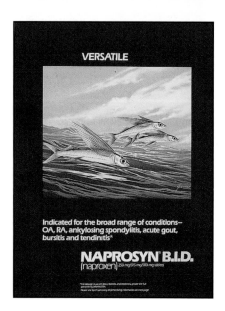

VERSATILE

Indicated for the broad range of conditions—
OA, RA, ankylosing spondylitis, acute gout,
bursitis and tendinitis*

NAPROSYN B.I.D.
(naproxen) 250 mg/375 mg/500 mg tablets

1 *CLIENT:* Syntex. *AGENCY:* Vicom/FCB.
AD: Joseph Rozon. *ILLUSTR.:* Will Nelson.
COPY: Cari Weisberg. **2** *CLIENT:* Smith Kline & French.
AGENCY: Salthouse Torre Norton.
AD: Mike Lazur. *COPY:* Mike Norton.
3 *CLIENT:* Boehringer Ingelheim.
AGENCY: Barnum. *AD:* Monica Garb.
ILLUSTR.: Alex Grey. *COPY:* Melissa de Fiebre.

GENTLE

Well-tolerated arthritis therapy*

NAPROSYN B.I.D.
(naproxen) 250 mg/375 mg/500 mg tablets

*The most frequently reported side effects relate to the G.I. tract.
Please see brief summary of prescribing information on next page.

1

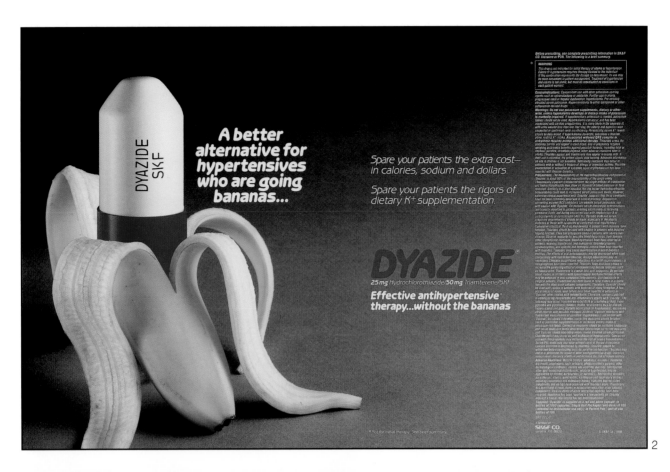

1 *CLIENT:* Pfizer. *AGENCY:* Dorritie & Lyons.
AD: Thomas Velardi *COPY:* Carol Shepko (1984).
2 *CLIENT:* Roche. *AGENCY:* McAdams.
AD: Carl Opalek. *COPY:* John Avery.
3 *CLIENT:* Glaxo Roche. *AGENCY:* McAdams.
CD: Walter Scott. *AD:* Chris Lella. *COPY:* Kevin McShane.

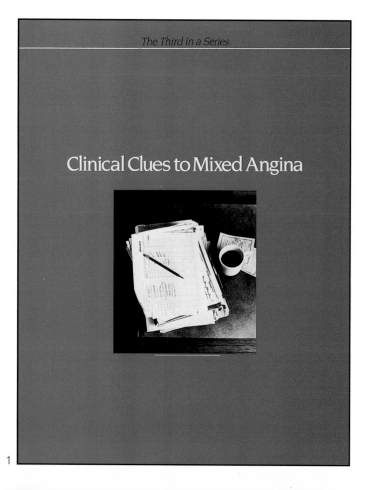

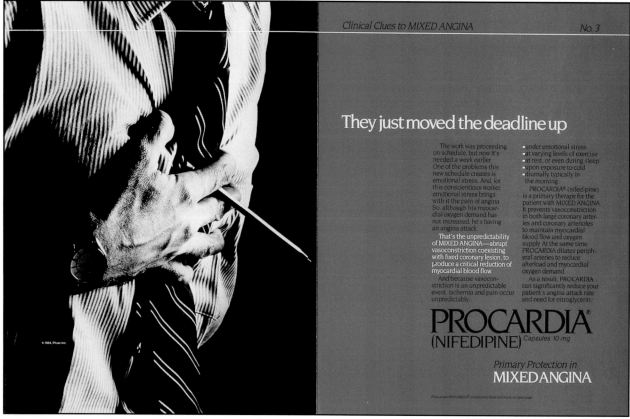

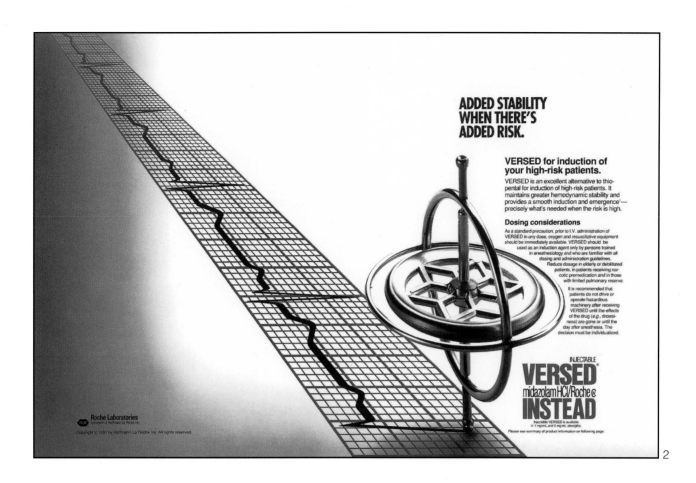

F E L D E N E ®
(piroxicam)

© 1985, Pfizer Inc.

It helps make arthritic   joints more articulate.

- Not only do joints move more easily, with less stiffness and swelling, but Feldene also provides prompt, long-lasting relief of pain and inflammation.[1]

- Convenient, once-daily dosage provides round-the-clock relief of symptoms[2]—encourages compliance and enhances productivity at home and on the job.[3]

- The most common side effects of Feldene are GI related. Other side effects (as indicated in the prescribing information) include dizziness, somnolence, vertigo, tinnitus, headache, malaise, edema, pruritus and rash.

Start one-a-day

Feldene® **For full**
(PIROXICAM) 20 mg **anti-**
capsules **arthritic**
action

Please see a brief summary of FELDENE (piroxicam) prescribing information on the following page.

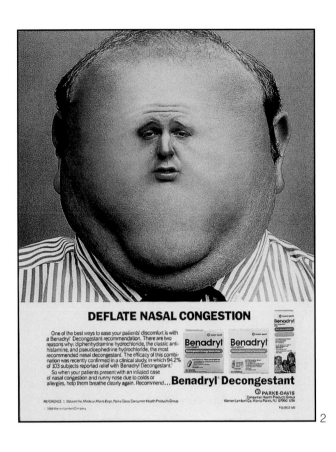

DEFLATE NASAL CONGESTION

One of the best ways to ease your patients' discomfort is with a Benadryl Decongestant recommendation. There are two reasons why: diphenhydramine hydrochloride, the classic anti-histamine, and pseudoephedrine hydrochloride, the most recommended nasal decongestant. The efficacy of this combi-nation was recently confirmed in a clinical study, in which 94.2% of 103 subjects reported relief with Benadryl Decongestant.

So when your patients present with an inflated case of nasal congestion and runny nose due to colds or allergies, help them breathe clearly again. Recommend... **Benadryl Decongestant**

PARKE-DAVIS
Consumer Health Products Group
Warner-Lambert Co. Morris Plains, NJ 07950 USA

2

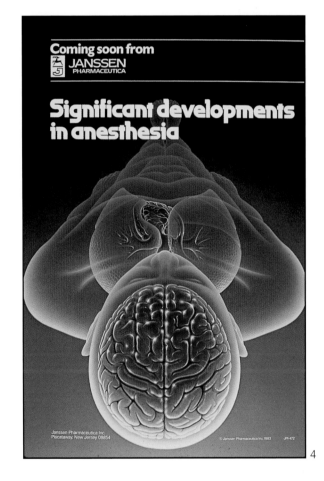

Coming soon from
JANSSEN PHARMACEUTICA

Significant developments in anesthesia

Janssen Pharmaceutica Inc.
Piscataway, New Jersey 08854

4

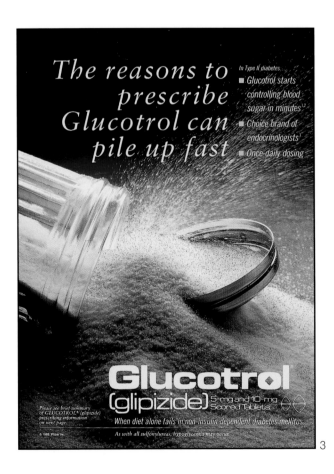

The reasons to prescribe Glucotrol can pile up fast

In Type II diabetes
■ Glucotrol starts controlling blood sugar in minutes
■ Choice brand of endocrinologists
■ Once-daily dosing

Glucotrol
(glipizide) 5-mg and 10-mg Scored Tablets

Please see brief summary of GLUCOTROL (glipizide) prescribing information on next page.

When diet alone fails in non-insulin-dependent diabetes mellitus

As with all sulfonylureas, hypoglycemia may occur.

3

1 *CLIENT:* Pfizer. *AGENCY:* Dorritie & Lyons.
AD: Mike Lyons. *PHOTOG:* Al Francevich.
COPY: Bill Brown (1985). **2** *CLIENT:* Parke-Davis.
AGENCY: Sudler & Hennessey.
AD: Ernie Smith. *PHOTOG.:* Ken & Carl Fischer.
COPY: Sandra Holtzman (1988).
3 *CLIENT:* Pfizer. *AGENCY:* Cline Davis & Mann.
AD: Clyde Davis. *COPY:* Ed Wise. (1989).
4 *CLIENT:* Janssen. *AGENCY:* Kallir, Philips, Ross.
AD: John Geryak. *ILLUSTR.:* Earl Kwam.

HYPERTENSION
IS USUALLY SILENT

CLIENT: Merck. *AGENCY:* FCB Healthcare.

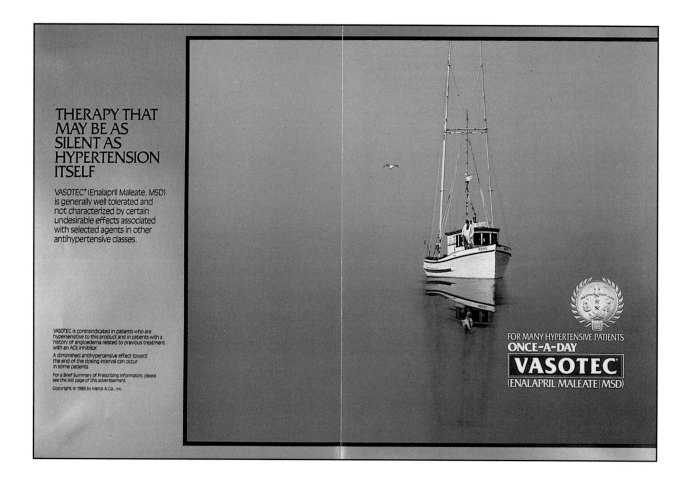

THERAPY THAT MAY BE AS SILENT AS HYPERTENSION ITSELF

VASOTEC® (Enalapril Maleate, MSD) is generally well tolerated and not characterized by certain undesirable effects associated with selected agents in other antihypertensive classes.

VASOTEC is contraindicated in patients who are hypersensitive to this product and in patients with a history of angioedema related to previous treatment with an ACE inhibitor.

A diminished antihypertensive effect toward the end of the dosing interval can occur in some patients.

For a Brief Summary of Prescribing information, please see the last page of this advertisement.

Copyright © 1989 by Merck & Co., Inc.

FOR MANY HYPERTENSIVE PATIENTS
ONCE–A–DAY
VASOTEC
(ENALAPRIL MALEATE | MSD)

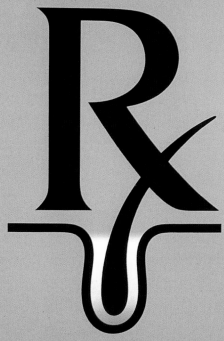

NEW
Rogaine®
TOPICAL SOLUTION — minoxidil 2%

THE FIRST PRESCRIPTION MEDICATION
PROVED EFFECTIVE
FOR MALE PATTERN BALDNESS
OF THE VERTEX

Upjohn

The Upjohn Company, Kalamazoo, Michigan 49001, USA

Please see adjacent page for brief summary of prescribing information.

© 1988 The Upjohn Company

J-9081
August 1988

CLIENT: Upjohn. AGENCY: Klemtner. CD: Tom Domanico.
AD/Designer: Julie Kenley. COPY: Liz Hevey.

1 CLIENT: Oral-B. AGENCY: Rainoldi Kerzner Radcliffe.
AD: Paschal Sabatella. PHOTOG: Ernie Friedlander.
COPY: Jeremiah Treacy.
2 CLIENT: Cooper Vision IOL. AGENCY: Gross Townsend
Frank & Hoffman. AD: Debra Prymus. ILLUS: Sister Corita

The 90's

Recession and Rebound

Uncertainty about new federal healthcare legislation, as well as the rapid growth of managed care, prompted a decline in promotional expenditures. However, when the proposed legislation failed in Congress, while managed care formularies proved less restrictive than anticipated, the industry responded with renewed energy and promotional activity.

Rx Advertising Weathers Promotional Downturn

From the mid 1950's, when the pharmaceutical renaissance began, until 1993, manufacturers' expenditures in advertising, promotion and communication programs had grown steadily. Field forces had gone from hundreds to thousands of representatives and journal ads from single-page displays of product packaging to colorful multi-page units. Sustained, over the years by pharmaceutical advertising, hundreds of medical publications were founded for general practice and specialty audiences which provided for the informational needs of physicians as medicine became more and more complex. An array of new promotional vehicles were created: advertising on Rx pads and health record forms; audio and video tapes for car, office and home; cable TV; FM radio; instructional programs in a variety of formats, all aimed at registering the industry's messages with prescribers. The remarkable growth in U.S. pharmaceutical sales from $1.3 billion in 1954[11] to $54.8 billion in 1994[12] supported the burgeoning growth in advertising and promotion.

Then in 1993, the virtually straight-line trend of some 40 years encountered new, threatening circumstances. The unrelenting rise in healthcare cost became a pressing concern for individuals and businesses and this concern translated into a political movement to restructure the health delivery system. In the debate over healthcare, the prices of pharmaceuticals were pushed center stage as a major part of the problem. New providers—managed care organizations (MCOs) and pharmaceutical benefit managers (PBMs)—emerged as cost-saving answers. Most importantly, the pharmaceutical industry, suddenly under pressure to hold down prices and envisioning a dramatically changing sales environment, pulled back on promotion. Advertising and promotional expenditures, along with all budgetary items (including research), came under scrutiny and with everything else, were reduced.

For example, the industry's overall field force size declined by 12% by the end of 1994. Journal advertising fell by almost 11% in 1993 and 3% in 1994.[13] However, counter-trend during this period, DTC experienced healthy growth—from $183 to $250 million in 1994.[14]

PROMOTIONAL REBOUND

The reduced spending of 1993 to 1994 proved to be short lived. The movement toward greater governmental control of healthcare finance and delivery was defeated in Congress. Companies learned how to market to managed care and the restrictive drug formularies predicted at MCOs failed to materialize as physicians resisted controls on their prescribing and patients showed preference for brand name pharmaceuticals. Also, as had happened in the past, the industry's research departments delivered new, important products that were immediately in demand. The result was a promotional recovery that began in 1995 and a continuation of the trend in Rx promotional growth into the late 1990's.

CLIENT: Roche. *AGENCY:* McAdams. *AD:* Mike Cummo. *Copy:* Claire Hakun (A rare example of an ad identifying with a physician's—rather than a patient's—daily routine) (1993).

GEOGRAPHIC DISPERSION

Many of today's agencies specializing in pharmaceutical advertising are now located well beyond the confines of Madison Avenue. The Chicago area has always been a focus of activity and remains so with such agencies as Abelson-Taylor, Corbett HealthConnect, Donahoe & Purohit, Goble, Hamilton Communications, McCann Healthcare, Sturm Rosenberg King, Topin, and Williams-Labadie.

Another major area for medical agencies is New Jersey, which is situated in close proximity to New York and the many Rx companies located in that state. These include the BHS Group, Catalyst Communications, CommonHealth, Cummings McFail & Nutry, Paul A. DeJesse, Dugan / Farley, Harrison Wilson, Integrated Communications, Lanmark Group, Bruce Leeb, Lewis Gace, Edward Newland, Pace, Ribotsky, Simms & McIvor, Strategic Medical and Torre Lazur.

In Northern California are Lena Chow, Fair Reily Call, FCB Healthcare, a branch office of Harrison Wilson and Sperling Sampson West, and in Southern California Baxter Gurian & Mazzei, BioGenesis, Esprit, Forsythe Marcelli Johnson, Lawrence & Mayo, and Pacific Communications.

Boston and environs are represented by BBK, Lehman Millet and Grob Scientific. In Philadelphia and nearby areas of Pennsylvania are Camp + Tate, Dorland Sweeney Jones, Dudnyk, Kingswood, Hal Lewis, K. I. Lipton, Toltzis, 30 West Advertising, and Vox (formerly Ted Thomas). Connecticut is home to Bryan Brown & Maynard, KSP Communications, and Leverte Associates.

To add to the industry's geographic range, medical agencies are operating throughout the U.S.: Atlanta—Adair Greene; Hollywood, FL—AD-TECH; Indianapolis—Communico; Durham, NC—Sandler & Recht; Raleigh, NC—Rockett Burkhead Lewis & Winslow; Arlington, TX—Saunders-Ream; Irvington, NY—Carrafiello-Diehl; Columbus, OH—Gerbig Snell / Weisheimer; and St. Louis—Atkinson Group.

Never let your guard down™

Orimune®
Poliovirus Vaccine Live
Oral Trivalent

32 years of proven polio protection

- Has helped virtually eliminate wild-type polio in the United States*

- Over 600 million doses distributed to date

- Uninterrupted supply since 1963

Trust a proven protector™

Manufactured by:
Lederle Laboratories
Division American Cyanamid Company
Pearl River, NY 10965

Marketed by:
WYETH-LEDERLE VACCINES AND PEDIATRICS
Wyeth-Ayerst Laboratories
Philadelphia, PA 19101

©1995, Wyeth-Ayerst Laboratories

* Paralytic disease following ingestion of live poliovirus vaccines has been reported on rare occasions in individuals receiving the vaccine or in their close contacts.

Please see brief summary of Prescribing Information on the following page.

66013

1

1 *CLIENT:* Wyeth-Lederle. *AGENCY:* Dugan/Farley.
COPY: Ilicia Scharfstein. *AD:* Jerry Kripscher.
2 *CLIENT:* Wyeth. *AGENCY:* Robert A Becker.
COPY: John Avery. *AD:* Andy Moore. (1995)

2

CLIENT: Abbott. AGENCY: Abelson-Taylor.
AD: Stephen Neale.
COPY: Jeff Chouinard. (1993).

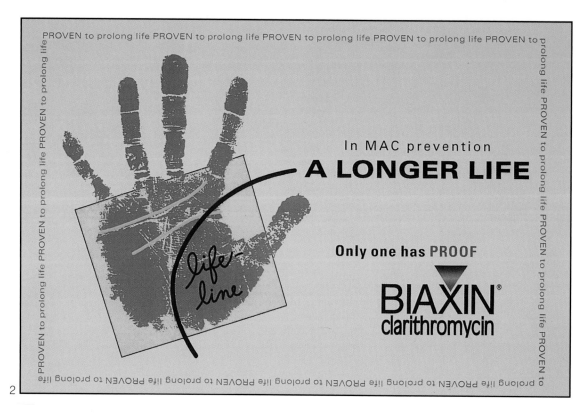

1 *CLIENT:* Sandoz. *AGENCY:* Integrated Communications.
AD: Johnathan Male. *COPY:* Charles DeMarco.
2 *CLIENT:* Abbott. *AGENCY:* Common Health.
3 *CLIENT:* Sandoz. *AGENCY:* Integrated Communications.
AD: Lin Kossak. *PHOTOG:* John Cooper.
COPY: Charles DeMarco. (1991)

CLIENT: Pfizer/Eisai. AGENCY: Lyons
Lavey Nickel Swift. AD: Peter Zamiska.
COPY: Todd Neuhaus/John Nosta.

102

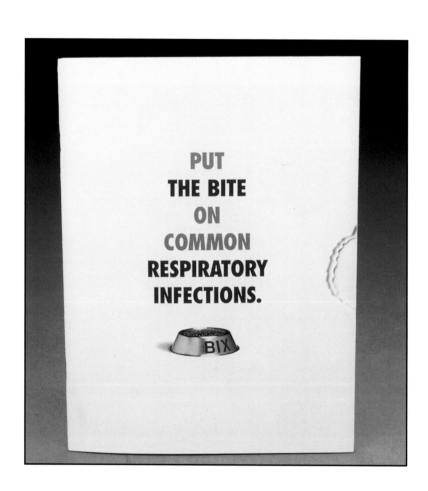

CLIENT: Abbott. AGENCY: Abelson-Taylor.
AD: Jan Podjasek. PHOTOG: Steve Grubman.
COPY: Pam Bryan.

HELP AVOID GLASSES IN LATER LIFE.

Now, dentists have a new screening exam called PSR™.
It's specially designed for early detection of gum disease —
a leading cause of tooth loss in adults. And it's fast and easy.
So help give your smile a healthy future…

ASK YOUR DENTIST ABOUT PSR

Periodontal Screening & Recording™

From the American Dental Association and
The American Academy of Periodontology.
Sponsored by Procter & Gamble Oral Care Products.

Periodontal Screening and Recording and PSR are service marks
and trademarks of the American Dental Association.
© 1995 by the American Dental Association and
The American Academy of Periodontology

ADA.

1

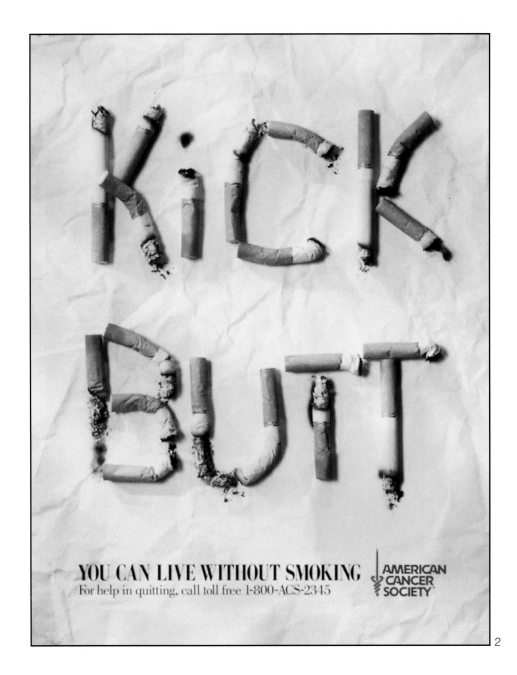

1

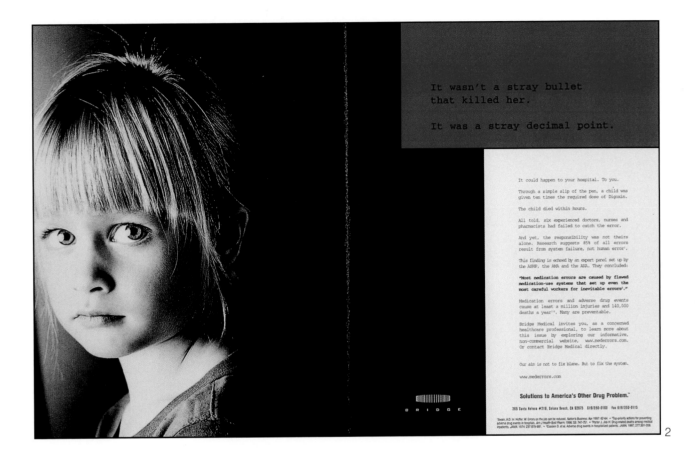

It wasn't a stray bullet
that killed her.

It was a stray decimal point.

It could happen to your hospital. To you.

Through a simple slip of the pen, a child was
given ten times the required dose of Digoxin.

The child died within hours.

All told, six experienced doctors, nurses and
pharmacists had failed to catch the error.

And yet, the responsibility was not theirs
alone. Research suggests 85% of all errors
result from system failure, not human error[1].

This finding is echoed by an expert panel set up by
the ASHP, the AMA and the AHA. They concluded:

"Most medication errors are caused by flawed
medication-use systems that set up even the
most careful workers for inevitable errors[2]."

Medication errors and adverse drug events
cause at least a million injuries and 140,000
deaths a year[3,4]. Many are preventable.

Bridge Medical invites you, as a concerned
healthcare professional, to learn more about
this issue by exploring our informative,
non-commercial website, www.mederrors.com.
Or contact Bridge Medical directly.

Our aim is not to fix blame. But to fix the system.

www.mederrors.com

Solutions to America's Other Drug Problem.™

285 Santa Helena #219, Solana Beach, CA 92075 619/350-0100 Fax 619/350-0115

2

1 *CLIENT:* Roche. *AGENCY:* Sudler & Hennessey.
AD: Arthur Kaufman *COPY:* Diane Cooney.
2 *CLIENT:* Bridge Medical *AGENCY:* Esprit Communications.
CD: Alan Proctor *AD:* Cassie Reich.
COPY: Leland Rosemond and Alan Proctor.

THE MODERN MEDICAL ADVERTISING AGENCY

M edical agencies will follow the scientific tradition advocated by Dr. Fishbein today and continuing into the next century. But they are now much more than ad makers who translate the medical literature into "logical" product messages. They have become diversified organizations providing more than advertising and sales force materials. Their divisions are now involved in medical education, sales training, public relations to professional and lay audiences, Internet programs, consumer advertising, international campaigns, corporate design and strategic planning—all activities required in a competitive climate for marketing success.

These kinds of services, as well as basic professional advertising, are in demand because, once again, the pharmaceutical industry is in the midst of an upswing. The government and managed care have recognized that the therapeutic efficiency of pharmaceuticals is essential to controlling healthcare costs. The Rx industry has also benefited from the Prescription Drug Users Fee Act (PDUFA) which provided for additional review staff at the FDA and accordingly more rapid approvals, putting more new, improved products on the market. Revised regulations on DTC advertising have also contributed to an optimistic promotional atmosphere.

Pharmaceuticals, with their biotech component, are part of the technological achievements that are propelling the American economy. Medical agencies are again in the forefront in communicating the news of beneficial and life saving products to healthcare professionals and the public. Pharmaceutical marketing will continue to build from basic promotion to healthcare professionals, to include programs directed to managed care management on costs and clinical outcomes, to extend to international markets where the communication common denominator will be medical science, and to reach the public with product message in consumer language. This complicated, interacting, informational mosaic will need to be designed by an informed and creative command center—a role medical agencies are equipped to play

MEDICAL ADVERTISING

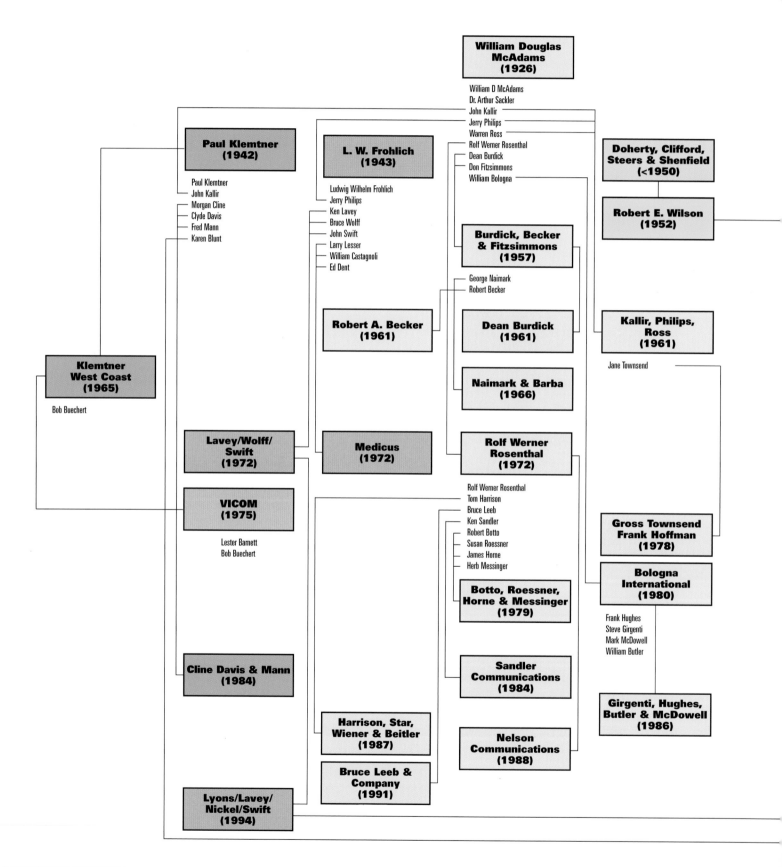

William Douglas McAdams (1926)

William D McAdams
Dr. Arthur Sackler
John Kallir
Jerry Philips
Warren Ross
Rolf Werner Rosenthal
Dean Burdick
Don Fitzsimmons
William Bologna

Paul Klemtner (1942)

Paul Klemtner
John Kallir
Morgan Cline
Clyde Davis
Fred Mann
Karen Blunt

L. W. Frohlich (1943)

Ludwig Wilhelm Frohlich
Jerry Philips
Ken Lavey
Bruce Wolff
John Swift
Larry Lesser
William Castagnoli
Ed Dent

Doherty, Clifford, Steers & Shenfield (<1950)

Robert E. Wilson (1952)

Burdick, Becker & Fitzsimmons (1957)

George Naimark
Robert Becker

Robert A. Becker (1961)

Dean Burdick (1961)

Kallir, Philips, Ross (1961)

Klemtner West Coast (1965)

Bob Buechert

Naimark & Barba (1966)

Jane Townsend

Lavey/Wolff/ Swift (1972)

Medicus (1972)

Rolf Werner Rosenthal (1972)

VICOM (1975)

Lester Barnett
Bob Buechert

Rolf Werner Rosenthal
Tom Harrison
Bruce Leeb
Ken Sandler
Robert Botto
Susan Roessner
James Horne
Herb Messinger

Gross Townsend Frank Hoffman (1978)

Bologna International (1980)

Frank Hughes
Steve Girgenti
Mark McDowell
William Butler

Botto, Roessner, Horne & Messinger (1979)

Cline Davis & Mann (1984)

Sandler Communications (1984)

Girgenti, Hughes, Butler & McDowell (1986)

Harrison, Star, Wiener & Beitler (1987)

Nelson Communications (1988)

Bruce Leeb & Company (1991)

Lyons/Lavey/ Nickel/Swift (1994)

AGENCY FOUNDERS TREE

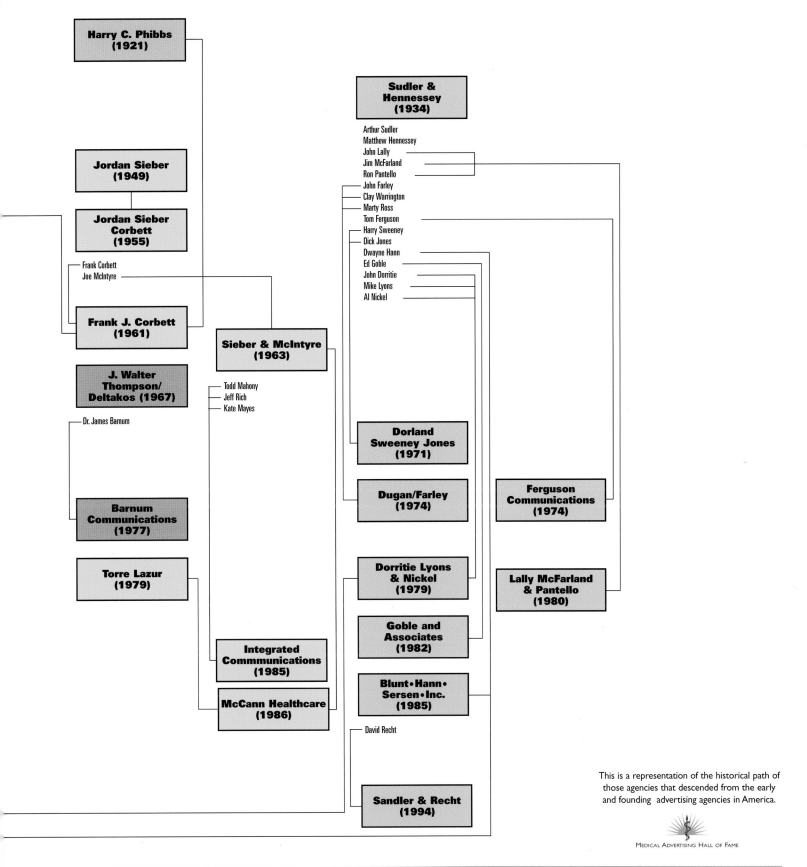

This is a representation of the historical path of those agencies that descended from the early and founding advertising agencies in America.

MEDICAL ADVERTISING HALL OF FAME

References

1. Starr, Paul, *The Social Transformation of American Medicine*, Basic Books, 1949.
2. Phibbs, Harry C. Note to Dr. Fishbein, Dr. Morris Fishbein Papers, The Joseph Regenstein Library, The University of Chicago.
3. Fishbein, Morris, MD, *How Advertising Helps Medicine Help the Public*, Printers' Ink, August 19, 1926.
4. Blum, Susan, *Agency Profiles—Sudler & Hennessey, Part I*, Medical Advertising News, February 15, 1984.
5. Ibid.
6. Enloe, Cortez, F., MD, *Advertising Agency Defined*, Pharmaceutical Marketing Orientation and Seminar, Rutgers—The State University College of Pharmacy Extension Service and The Pharmaceutical Advertising Club of New York, 1955.
7. Wagner, Tobias, *Ethical Pharmaceutical Promotion*, The Workings and Philosophies of the Pharmaceutical Industry, National Pharmaceutical Council, 1959.
8. Hearings, Subcommittee on Antitrust and Monopoly of the Committee of the Judiciary United States Senate, December 7, 1959.
9. Cray, William C., *The Pharmaceutical Manufacturers Association—The First 30 Years*, Pharmaceutical Manufacturers Association, 1988.
10. Hearings, Subcommittee on Antitrust and Monopoly of the Committee of the Judiciary United States Senate, January 30, 31, and February 1, 1962.
11. U.S., Department of Commerce.
12. Pharmaceutical Research and Manufacturers of America.
13. Scott-Levin Associates, *Sales Force Structure and Strategies*, 1994.
14. Leading National Advertisers, *Media Watch Multi-Media Service*, 1994.

TYPOGRAPHY:

Text: 11/20 Carmina Light
    with 16/20 Carmina Bold Italic heads

Calligraphy: designed and hand-rendered
    by Tom Carnese

PRINTING:

Oceanic Graphic Printing Ltd.
Paper stock:
    interior—128 gsm Matt Art
    dust jacket—157 gsm Glossy Art

Text Index

Creative Index